MW01265145

For my big

Lyn

Living in Nicaragua and Other Countries

Also, by H. Lynn Beck

1.   Henry and Anthony, Second Edition

2.   Living in Brazil

3.   Living in El Salvador

CONTENTS

How It Started

I graduated with a degree in agriculture from the University of Nebraska at Lincoln in May 1971; yet, I was dissatisfied, unhappy, and without goals. I always thought college graduates should know what they wanted to do in life. Not me, I was confused, likely from the two years I had spent in the Peace Corps in El Salvador from 1967 to 1969. That experience had changed me profoundly and I was having difficulty dealing with those changes.

I still suffered from reverse culture shock--the inability to adjust to one's native culture after returning from an extended stay in a foreign culture. I no longer felt at home in the US. I always felt on edge and irritated. There were many reasons for this.

I had spent the last two years living with students at the University of Nebraska. To me, many of these students felt entitled, ungrateful, and unaware of the world's dark side. For example, I felt that they wasted food at the cafeteria and were picky about what they ate, always complaining about the quality of the food. For me, the food was excellent and available in unimaginable quantities. They had never been hungry for more than a few hours. Food always tastes good to a hungry person and there is never enough of it. I had seen too many hungry and desperate people to not appreciate it.

These students were in college, which was only a dream to most young people in third world countries where most children don't study beyond the sixth grade. Yet, at the university, many students skipped class and did not pay attention when they went to class. To me, these were unforgivable sins for someone who had a chance of a lifetime. I had met so many young people in El Salvador that would have fought for an opportunity to go to the university. Almost anyone could enter a US university, yet students seemed not to value the opportunity that our society was giving us.

From what I could see, most students had limitless closets full of shirts, blouses, shoes, shorts, and coats. In El Salvador, I knew many people who had two or three changes of clothes, at most. Many had only the clothes on their bodies. That was a fact of life. There was no complaining because complaining did not produce more food or clothes.

In addition, to reverse culture shock, I had no confidence in my technical ability as a college graduate. Before I joined the Peace Corps, I had had misgivings about how applicable what I had learned at the university was. When I returned from the Peace Corps, my hope was that the last two years at the university would pull my learning together and make me feel competent. It did not happen. I always went to class. I studied and I asked questions, but in the end, I was left with a feeling of disappointment in myself and in the curriculum that I studied.

I had always imagined that a university degree would provide one with the knowledge that could open the secrets of the universe. I was wrong again. Later, I learned that the university provided the necessary foundation. What I lacked was practical experience. No amount of technical knowledge can compensate for a lack of experience.

I didn't look for a job in agriculture. Instead, I looked for work at the Lincoln Regional Center--a state-run institution for troubled minds. I was hired to work with boys with emotional problems aged twelve to seventeen. Most of the boys had serious emotional problems; although, they often seemed normal. There was no chance of advancement in this job, but maybe, it would give me time to find myself and choose a direction in life that would be more compatible with my personality.

At work, we always had to be on guard. When one child became nervous, for whatever reason, he could cause the others to feed on that nervousness. The result could be a sudden shift in the collective mood from one of peacefulness to danger.

One evening there were only two of us on duty. My colleague was hired in the same batch as I was. We both had the same experience, and neither had much verbal control over the patients. We took our group to recreation in the basement. Some patients were playing basketball, others played pool, and still, others were standing around. It was our job to keep everyone engaged. We encouraged the idle clients to find something to do. Suddenly, they tired of our insistence that they engage and became angry. Their mood changed quickly, and they raised their voices and started to become aggressive. From one minute to the next, we were in a serious bind. We had thirteen angry male teenagers ganging up on two inexperienced employees. One boy picked up a couple of pool balls, one in each hand, and started swinging them around threateningly, while another couple of boys picked up pool cues and started to bang one end in their other hand. The boy with the pool balls challenged me to make them do what they didn't want to do. The others came closer and stared at me to see how I was going to react.

My colleague slipped into the office and called the second-floor section that managed another group of male patients. As luck would have it, they also only had two employees. It was against state law for either of us to work with fewer than two employees; therefore, he could not legally leave his post to help us. My colleague gave me the bad news as we tried to figure out how to deal with our problem.

Before we knew what was happening, our friend from the second floor burst open the entrance doors, which I knew was for show, stopped, placed his hands on his hips, and looked from one boy to another without saying a word. This employee was a long-time employee and had instant respect from our patients. They surrendered, and we took them all to Quiet Rooms on the first and second floors and locked them up for the remainder of the shift. These Quiet Rooms were about eight by nine feet and had no light bulbs. Light bulbs could be broken, and the clients could use them to harm themselves. The windows were covered by bars and screens to protect the clients. I still give thanks to the second floor's employee's help.

I didn't like working at the Center, but each morning I had a destination and at the end of every two weeks, I had a paycheck. It was one way of treading water while I was in my completely confusing stage of life.

After a few months, I realized that I needed to look for a better job. I began to summarize the strengths and weaknesses of what I did in the Peace Corps when I worked as an Agricultural Extension Agent. I liked doing that. If I were successful at teaching a peasant farmer a new agricultural technique, he and his family were less hungry the following year. That was positive reinforcement. I wanted to decrease hunger. I wanted to work in Latin America.

I started thinking about the many ways that I, personally, could work to decrease hunger. I thought about the shortcomings of the agricultural extension system. Traveling to all the different villages took time, and without a vehicle, we could only visit one village per day. Running around the villages trying to find people to work with also took time. It took time to find people willing to allow us to establish an experiment on their property. These farmers had such small plots of land with which to produce the following year's food that they were usually hesitant to cede any of it to be used in an experiment. I was hesitant to encourage them to change their production method because it could fail and because the peasant family great harm. Sometimes, for whatever reason, experiments failed. This could significantly reduce their total food production and allow hunger into the household.

I began thinking of another way of dispensing useful knowledge to the peasant farmers. I thought about an agricultural school. It would have a fixed location with fixed and well developed experiments. It could have many small enterprises: a couple of cows, a few pigs, a few chickens, both to lay eggs and for meat production, some corn, black beans, bananas, and other crops. If an experiment failed, our farm suffered, but no peasant would feel hunger because of it. It would be cheaper to bring a dozen peasant farmers, and/or their children, the future peasant farmers, to the farm than to develop these projects in each of dozens of communities. We could use a bus or van to bring them to the school for a day's show and tell, or we could bring young people, future farmers, to the school for them to do an internship for a few weeks or months. We might even create a certificate that they could obtain if they completed a prescribed course at the farm.

That was it! I would create an Agricultural School Project and then try to find a place to apply it. I developed the project on paper and sent it around to organizations that I thought could benefit from such a project. For months there was no response, then, one day, I received a letter from the First Baptist Church in Cleveland, Ohio. They were associated with a church group that owned approximately eighty acres of land on the edge of Managua, Nicaragua. They asked if I would be interested in knowing more. Oh, yes, I would.

The Baptist churches in Managua were active. They had a Baptist School and a Baptist Hospital that were considered the best in Nicaragua. The school, the hospital, and the church were all started through the leadership of Dr. Arturo Parajón. His son, Dr. Gustavo Parajón continued his father's work as a physician in the hospital and as an elder in the church. If I were to work in Managua, Dr. Parajón would provide any medical care that I might need for free. The farm had a nice house that the church would also occasionally use for meetings but graciously allowed me to live there for free. The church had a fund that could pay me forty-five dollars a month. As a comparison, Peace Corps Volunteers in Managua earned one hundred dollars a month. My lifestyle would have to be modest, much more so than the one I had led as a Peace Corps volunteer in El Salvador.

The Baptist church in Nicaragua encouraged all young members to provide one year of service to a rural community after they graduated from high school. The church also received groups from its associated church in Cleveland, Ohio during the summer. They went to a rural community and worked for its betterment.

For me, the decision was easy: new adventures in Nicaragua, or continue to work with twelve to seventeen-year-old problematic children. I was not good at working with these children. I was not bad at my job, but I had colleagues who had developed a rapport with the children and could maintain control over them. That was our job: to control them. I notified the Cleveland First Baptist Church that I accepted their offer.

I prepared for my trip. I already had a passport. I obtained a visa and packed my bags and a trunk. I had just bought a high-quality stereo set with wonderful speakers. I decided that if I were going to rough it, I could do so while listening to my music. I took my trunk and the boxes with my stereo to the Post Office and mailed them to Nicaragua via ship. It would take a few weeks to reach me. I could not afford to have them shipped by air.

The day arrived for my departure, and again, I was going to the airport, but this time my sister took me, not the entire family, as when I left for my first Peace Corps tour. She waited with me at the airport until my flight was called. We hugged and she left. I boarded the plane and found a seat in the back. I was again left to my thoughts. This time, I had no idea when I would return. The job had no ending date. I did not care. I wanted to speak Spanish again, and I wanted to confront the challenges of living and working in Latin America. I was ready for whatever might come.

I   Arrived in Managua

Juan, a young man with a wide smile and a bounce in his step, picked me up at the airport. He kept the conversation flowing as he drove to the farm using the one-hand-on-the-wheel-and the other-on-the-horn method of driving. It seemed to be the most popular method used in Managua.

It had been the same in El Salvador, but to a lesser degree than it was in Managua. Drivers in Managua had mastered that driving style.

After driving several miles south from the airport, Juan turned left without warning from the highway onto a narrow dirt road. The road was not easily visible from the highway, at least, not to my untrained eyes. There was a vine with purple flowers growing from one side of the road entrance. It grew up and over the entrance, making the dirt road even less evident from the highway. The narrow dirt road continued after the flowery entrance. Small houses were located on both sides of the street, but most were hidden behind either an adobe brick wall or a wire fence covered in flowers or bushes.

We drove just shy of a half-mile and turned right onto an even narrower path. This path was only wide enough for our Land Rover to pass between the overgrown brush and small trees growing in the fences located on both sides of the path. After a quarter-mile on this path, we turned left again. Here, I had to get out of the vehicle to open a barbed wire gate. The path led us to the farm property with a white farmhouse located on a hilltop overlooking the city of Managua. Just this side of the farmhouse was located a smaller storage shed. There were twenty or thirty beehives located on the far side of the house with a couple of large shade trees providing shade for some of the bees.

The house had a wonderfully large front porch that allowed people to sit and view the farm below it. The house had a bathroom and two bedrooms. I claimed the bedroom closer to the bathroom. The house also had a combination kitchen and dining area. There were many windows in the house providing a panoramic view of Managua which lies below us. The floor consisted of tiles that were cool to the touch of my bare feet. Juan placed a scissors cot for me in my chosen bedroom. We unloaded my suitcase and placed it in my bedroom. Juan then took me into the city to buy sheets, pillows, and other accessories that I needed.

Within the first week, I learned that I needed to make my bed every day. I stretched the sheets tight because I had luckily unmasked a large scorpion when I shook the upper sheet. That created a habit that I would never lose while I lived in Nicaragua--the daily shaking of the sheets. To that, I added the daily habit of holding each shoe upside down while shaking vigorously because, once, as I was about to put on my shoes, I heard a noise in my shoe. Curious, I looked inside but I did not see anything. I then turned the shoe upside down and shook it and a large black scorpion dropped out.

Juan introduced me to the current peasant farm manager--Don Luis (Don is a title of respect). He had been responsible for supervising the two or three workers who had been required to keep the farm running. Now, he would report to me. I would use him to oversee the workers in the field.

The field workers consisted of two adults and a seventeen-year-old. All field workers struggled with their reading, writing, and arithmetic. They could write their names and read a little. The boy, Julio, could also perform a few calculations. Because I wanted to start to collect data to determine the cost of production for everything we produced, I would require one of the workers to keep track of how many hours each worker spent performing each task during the week. Don Luis could not do this because numbers confused him. The record keeper, in addition to his regular work, would need to weigh every item harvested and know from which field it came. I needed at least one worker to be good with numbers in addition to reading and writing. I thought that it would be Julio. He showed the most enthusiasm when I discussed what was needed with the workers.

The First Baptist Church worked to fight illiteracy. The church created learning centers around the country. In these centers, local community leaders helped teach the illiterate to read and write by using teaching methods that the church had developed or adapted from other people's work. I wanted to apply these teaching methods and use their materials on the farm for the workers who were interested in improving their reading, writing, and mathematics skills.

When I presented this option to the workers, they all opted into the program. We agreed that we would do this after work each day at the farmhouse. On the first day, the workers were all present and excited. We found some school desks inside the house's dining area. I brought them out onto the porch. I explained the program to the workers and gave each worker his personal book and a pencil to use. They worked at their own pace. I drifted among them to give them encouragement. They were timid and would not ask questions at first, but later, they became less intimidated. No one showed more excitement than Julio.

While the workers were studying alone, I developed worksheets on which we would collect data. One documented the crops produced and the areas of each. Another documented how the workforce's time was used: how many hours were devoted to executing each task for each crop. After becoming satisfied with each form, I redrew it and showed it to Julio. The next day he would start to collect data. He was so enthusiastic that he gave me a smile that was so wide that it engulfed his ears.

For work, we started producing a few vegetables. Since the rains had not yet come, we only planted a small area. Without rain, the seedlings needed to be irrigated every couple of days. We only had water from our house pump and a garden hose. This limited the scale of our operations.

We had to think about how we should market the products. Nearby was a modern hotel in which Howard Hughes was reportedly occupying the seventh floor. I thought that perhaps we could obtain the highest price there for our quality vegetables. We established the hotel as our primary market. Because we had no vehicle to carry our production, any overflow would go to the community market, which could be reached on foot; even though, their prices were lower.

The workers slept in our storage shed. They either did not have a home, or they lived too far away to commute, so they slept onsite. On weekends, they mostly disappeared. I did not ask questions.

The workers paid a cook to prepare their meals. Their meals were simple: mostly pasty spaghetti, eggs, rice, and black beans. Since I made about the same money as they did, I joined their group. We pooled our money and paid a cook to buy and prepare food for us.

At mealtime, the cook would call us. She always placed the food on a small wooden table under a large shade tree, located between the house and the shed. She prepared the food in the shed where the workers slept. She covered the food with a tablecloth to protect it from the swarms of flies that occupied the area. I learned that when we removed the tablecloth, we had to defend our food and fruit juice. We ate with our right hands and swatted flies with our left hands. It was an impossible job. If I swatted my food, a swarm of flies landed on my juice glass. If I swatted around the glass, a swarm of flies landed on my food. My workers were having no better luck.

The flies became such a problem that we agreed to take the tablecloth that had covered our food and fully unfold it. We then placed it over our heads creating an extra barrier between the flies and our food. That allowed us to eat while defending our plates and food, but that was not good enough. The flies were still finding our food and eating as much as we were. That is when I had the idea. I would take my knife and tap my juice glass. The ringing noise would surely scare the flies away. It worked for a few days, but then, more and more flies appeared. My only explanation was that the flies must have associated the glass ringing as a call to eat and came with that single purpose. In the end, our only defense was to swat fast and eat even faster. It must have appeared strange to anyone watching us eat: four men under a tablecloth with both arms moving rapidly in all directions.

The house and large tree came with a Lapa, a large colorful parrot. Mostly, he stayed in the tree and screeched. He had a very loud and shrill screech. It was very annoying. His favorite time to sing the song of his ancestors was at five in the morning. I couldn't sleep beyond that time. I could set my watch to the beast's morning screech. I hated that beast.

Sometimes he would climb down the tree, waddle to the shed next to the house, climb up the water gutters, and screech there for a while. If I was standing in the shade of the tree, he often climbed down the tree trunk, waddled to my leg, and climbed up using his beak. He grasped my pants with his beak and pulled himself up. He slowly and deliberately climbed my pants and then my shirt. If his beak found flesh under my pants, I screamed in pain, but my screams did not influence where he clasped his feet or his beak. He climbed until he was on my shoulder.

Sometimes he seemed so cute and cuddly. He stood on my shoulder and rubbed my ear with his beak. Then the evil devil would bite my ear with enough force to crack a walnut. I could not defend myself by knocking him down because he would have taken a piece of my ear with him. I had to apply pressure on his body by slowly increasing it until he released my ear. All the while, I had to be careful not to harm him. When freed, I threw him back into his tree. I had no idea why he was so mean.

Finally, I received a message from customs that my packages had arrived. I was elated. I wanted to listen to music on my stereo. Juan drove me to customs. I expected to sign a few papers and claim my things, but that was not the way it was done in Somoza's (the dictator) Nicaragua. I can no longer remember what the difficulty was, but something was wrong. I could not take my things until I did something. I really did not understand what the problem was. I was very unhappy. I had to turn and walk out of customs without my things. Juan said that he thought they were fishing for bribes to release my property.

When Dr. Parajón heard of this, he was able to clear part of his day's business schedule within a couple days and accompany me to customs. He straightened it out, and I walked out with my property without paying a bribe. Dr. Parajón was a well-known and highly respected man in Nicaragua. What I remember most about Dr. Parajón was that he was very soft-spoken.

His voice was so soft that everyone had to pay attention to hear him, yet they always heard him. Dr. Parajón was my hero. He was super-human. He was a force. He faced so many impossible problems each day, and somehow, he resolved them without raising his voice or saying a bad word about anyone. He was a true Christian.

Meanwhile, I was teaching Julio how to use the newly developed data collection forms to collect data. He had bought an inexpensive watch so that he could time the activities. He periodically took notes during the day to allow him to accurately fill in the forms at the end of the day. The idea was simple, but it was not easy to achieve with accuracy. It took us a couple of weeks before I was receiving usable data. I had never seen anyone respond to a few words of praise as much as Julio did. He was a delight to work with.

Each day, after work, we continued our literacy training. I was surprised by how excited the men were to learn after a hard day's work. They wanted to be able to read and write. Julio's training included mathematical problems so that he could calculate hours worked, each day's crop production, and overall totals.

Every night I prepared more data collection sheets because these were each hand prepared. I collected Julio's sheets and prepared summary sheets and shared my results with Julio, who was ecstatic to be included in the process. He loved to be learning new things and to be taken into my confidence when I shared the results with him. He loved the attention given to him.

Going to Panama to Buy a Motorcycle

I needed transportation. I was anchored at the farmhouse. For a twenty-five-year-old man, that was too confining. I looked at motorcycles in Managua, but they were expensive due to Nicaragua's high import taxes. That was when I remembered that the Panama Canal Zone was tax-free. I could buy a motorcycle in Panama tax-free. When I told Dr. Parajón of my plans, he informed me that when I brought the motorcycle into Nicaragua; I would still have to pay Nicaragua's import tax. He told me that, if I wanted to buy a cycle in the Canal Zone, he could produce a document declaring that the motorcycle would be used for the church's purposes, and then I would no longer need to pay import taxes. The only restriction he placed on me was that, should I leave the country, I would sell my cycle to someone doing the church's work.

I flew to Panama City and bought a Honda 350 cubic centimeter dirt bike and a helmet. It was wonderful. With my new cycle, I drove to a hardware store and bought six feet of heavy chain with a heavy-duty padlock to secure my cycle whenever I parked it. With this in hand, I started up the Pan American Highway. I couldn't believe that I could go anywhere I wanted, anytime I wanted. I fell in love with the rumble of my cycle's engine as I headed north toward Costa Rica.

Panama was a green country. Everywhere I looked, it was green. The Pan American highway ran through flatlands, but it was never far from the hills. I judged their distance by their blue hue: the closer vegetation was dark green while the farther from the highway; the deeper the blue hue.

It was relaxing to feel the cycle's vibration, hear the hum of the motor, and see the highway disappear under its wheels. I was not in a hurry. It was a moment I wanted to extend as much as possible. It was very cloudy, and rain was imminent, especially since the rainy season was already overdue. That was one disadvantage of being on a cycle--the exposure to the weather. I accelerated. The next city was David, a city located in north Panama and named after President Eisenhower. I hoped to reach it before the rain came.

The highway passed along the eastern edge of David. I noticed a rooming house sign next to an area surrounded by a high white wall. The rooming house was located inside the walls. I thought this would be a secure area for my motorcycle. I entered the compound and parked my cycle. I rented a room for the night and convinced the owner to allow me to park my cycle inside the house. She was a very understanding woman. Even so, I applied my chain and padlock. My cycle was a beautiful machine. I would not risk losing it.

The next morning, I ate breakfast and was off. I was only an hour from the Costa Rican border, which I reached without incident. The road from the border into San José was dirt with deep ruts left from last year's rainy season. These ruts could be catastrophic to a car, truck, or bus; but to a motorcycle, they could bring death. If either of my wheels were to fall into a deep rut, it could flip my cycle sideways or stop it in its tracks-- throwing me from the cycle. I had to avoid the deep ruts, or if they were unavoidable, I had to transverse them at an angle so that my wheels could cross the ruts without falling into them. This required me to drive very slowly or to think and react very quickly.

I entered Costa Rica and raised my bottom from the cycle's seat a little and supported my weight on my legs. This allowed me to increase my speed to a moderate level. I had to keep my eyes glued to the road to avoid my tire dropping into any ruts. After less than an hour, my cycle stopped suddenly. It did not sputter or make any conking sounds; it just stopped. All efforts to restart the cycle failed. I was devastated.

I was well inside a rain forest area of Costa Rica with a dead motorcycle. I pushed the cycle to the edge of the oversized road and thought. I had not seen any villages behind me. I had no idea what lay ahead of me. I started pushing my cycle, hoping the rainy season would hold off another couple of days. After a couple hours, a small truck stopped and asked if I needed help. I asked the driver where I could find a mechanic. He said that a few miles back there was a village a couple of miles off the road. He agreed to haul me and my cycle there--for a modest fee. I agreed.

The village had a mechanic, a market, a bank, and several other businesses. It was modest, but it was what I needed. They located the mechanic. He was twenty-something years old, had long greasy hair, a thin scraggly beard, and two teeth. He was wearing flip-flops, a greasy, torn shirt, and an old pair of pants. He had grease smudges on his arms, hands, and face. When he understood he was going to work on a new motorcycle, he took a step back, examined the cycle from stem to stern, and opened a broad smile that fully exposed both his teeth. At that moment, I felt that I was in deep trouble. I didn't think he had a clue how to repair a cycle. He explained that he wouldn't be able to complete any work until early the next day. Luckily for me, there was a small hotel in town, in fact, located almost next to the mechanic's shop. I rented a room from the hotel, found a simple restaurant, ordered chicken fried rice, and settled in for the night. I was grateful that I would spend the night in a cheap hotel rather than on the side of the road in a rain forest.

The next morning, I ate breakfast and walked to the mechanic's shop. I was resolved to stand and watch him work on my cycle, but that was unnecessary. I found that he had already made the repair. It was a sweet moment when I gave the cycle a slight crank and the motor responded. I was so happy that the motor started immediately that I did not ask him what the problem with it had been. I only asked him how much it was. I do not remember how much it was, but it was a reasonable amount. I tried to pay him in US dollars, but he only accepted Costa Rican money. I had to wait for the bank to open at 10:00 am, which did not make me happy. Once it opened, I exchanged the money, paid him, and pointed my cycle back toward the road from which I had come.

When I reached the Pan American highway again, I turned right and accelerated as I picked my path among the deep ruts. After an hour's journey, the cycle again stopped, and my heart accelerated. What the heck was going on? I had a new cycle. Again, in the middle of nowhere, I was pushing my cycle. Again, after a few hours, a truck appeared and stopped. They gave me and my cycle a ride up the road to a lone gas station that happened to have a mechanic. I accepted their kind offer.

After a few minutes, the truck driver pulled to the side of the road by a gas station. There was no village, just a gas station located on the side of the road. The owner was in the process of closing. I quickly paid the driver, unloaded my cycle, and pushed it toward the gas station attendant as fast as I could. I begged him not to close until he had looked at my cycle. My pleas did not move him. He was done for the day, and he closed despite my pleading for him to stay open and check my cycle. He said I could keep my cycle inside his building, and that he would look at it first thing in the morning, and he left me standing.

Darkness was but a few minutes away; I was hungry; I had no place to stay, and there was no village for many miles in any direction. I looked around and found an old, abandoned bus pushed off to the side of the road. It was mostly concealed by the jungle and consisted of only an old body. It had no wheels or motor, but the seats inside were still mostly intact, although most of the windows had been broken. I noticed that in the back, the windows and seats were still intact. That would be the safest place for me because no one could position themselves behind me. I walked to the back of the bus and situated my things under my seat and sat down. I tested the seat and was satisfied that I would be safe there. I tried to sleep and finally did, despite the many hungry mosquitos.

I awoke the next morning to find that most of the seating was occupied by other travelers and their merchandise. I grabbed my things and camped out in front of the gas station. After a few minutes, the owner arrived and opened the station. He started to work on my cycle. Within minutes he had found the problem. This motorcycle had a "kill" switch located next to my left hand handle. Its purpose, I think, was for the driver to hit it with his thumb if any dangerous or unstable situation arose, and that would kill the engine. Obviously, my thumb had hit it twice as I and my cycle bounced around the rough road. I felt like an idiot. He charged me an appropriate fee and I was back on the road--this time without any more unscheduled interruptions.

The dirt road ended just south of San José. With the aid of pavement, I made good time; although, my bottom was raw from the hours of riding on a cycle and bouncing all around. Even so, I was going to try to arrive in Nicaragua yet that day. With straight pavement, I could travel at high velocity with my 350 cubic centimeter cycle. I had no problem maintaining high speeds while climbing steep grades.

Midafternoon, I arrived at the Nicaraguan border only to find that, even as a permanent resident, I could not reenter Nicaragua without an entry visa. Luckily, I could obtain this at a consulate located one hour back in a regional city. I turned my cycle around and opened it up, quickly arriving at the consulate. I obtained my visa and was back at the Nicaraguan border lickity-split. The entire process only took a couple hours. Now, I had to hurry to make it home before dark, which I did.

Making Payroll

It felt good to be safely home with my beautiful new cycle. Now that I had my stereo, I could listen to music and, with my cycle, I had mobility. Life was good, even though it still had not rained. I was worried because everyone said that the rainy season in Nicaragua was already late.

Every Friday afternoon, I had to travel into Managua to cash the church's check for that week's payroll. In the bank, there was a beautiful, young and charming teller. She had jet black hair and always had a smile that reached all the way down to her soul. I always stood in her line, even if other tellers were available. She had to notice my strange behavior, but she did not say anything. She smiled when it was my turn for her to wait on me. She was very professional and efficient. I tried to delay the transaction if possible, to learn more about her, but that was not easy. She was friendly, but volunteered no personal information, even if there were no more clients in her line. As for pay day, I put the cash in a small backpack and took it to my house. For safety, I put it under my cot and pulled my sheet down to cover it.

Once a month, I went to a small hotel called La Florida to eat three blueberry pancakes with maple syrup. I always ate them slowly to extract every bit of flavor from them and to enjoy the air-conditioned environment. They were so good.

On an alternative weekend, also, once a month, I bought a banana split at an air-conditioned restaurant. I ate it as slowly as possible to maximize its savory taste, but I could not eat too slowly, or it would melt. That was all the luxury that I could afford each month, especially since I now had to set aside some money for gas for my beloved motorcycle.

One day, we received an encouraging rain that more than settled the dust. We were in the second year of drought; consequently, we were in a celebratory mood. I was driving my cycle to a bar to have a couple celebratory beers when I saw a Dutch friend in his yard. He was the master brewer at the largest brewery in Nicaragua. I stopped and we talked about the prospects of more rain. He was not optimistic. I was. Farmers must be optimistic. He invited me into his house to try a few beers. I carefully guided my cycle through his front yard gate and hid it behind shrubbery while he locked the gate. In his house, he handed me an all-copper mug and the coldest beer I had tasted in months. We drank several beers as he told me his story of traveling from Holland to Nicaragua. After a couple hours, I carefully drove back to my house.

Fortunately, my drive only required me to drive on narrow paths with no traffic.

Despite the short shower, most farmers were afraid to plant because the rains were late. When rains were late, they were often unreliable, but after today's rain, I was sure that the more optimistic farmers would start to plant more crops. For the remaining farmers, more rains would be required before they committed their cash to planting. They could not afford a false start. If they planted seed, applied fertilizer, and then the rains stopped; they would lose their investment.

I obtained permission to hire more workers to clear the weeds and brush in expectation of planting vegetables. I hired fifteen to twenty workers because, if the rains started for certain, we would be able to plant the seeds before the sun could dry the ground surface. I had to make sure that Don Luis kept a close eye on the number of workers that came each day. This was necessary because workers often disappeared for a day or two and then reappeared. In addition, I wanted to know what each worker did and how much work he accomplished. Don Luis and Julio needed to be on their toes. When it came time to lay off a few workers, we could lay off our less productive ones.

Friday at noon, Don Luis and I prepared the payroll sheet. For our calculations, we assumed that all workers would work Saturday morning. On Friday afternoon I went into Managua to the bank. The next day at noon, the men stopped work and gathered under the shade of the big tree. I pulled a small table and stool out onto the porch from inside the house and sat my backpack on the table. I arranged the bills in stacks by each denomination. I called the first man on the list. I confirmed with each man how many days he had worked and how much he had earned. If the man agreed, I counted the money and gave it to him to count, if he could count. If he was satisfied, he made an X on the line indicating that he had received his money and the line moved on.

As each man received his money, he disappeared quickly because he wanted to make it to Saturday market before all the good fruit and vegetables were sold. After the payroll was completed, I climbed on my cycle and headed to visit a friend or to buy my banana split or blue berry pancakes. Sometimes, I just rode around to hear my motorcycle's engine when I accelerated and to feel the engine's vibration.

Traffic in Managua was dangerous, especially for someone riding a motorcycle. Drivers failed to respect signs and signals.

They did not even consider them as a strong suggestion. You could never assume that a green light meant that you could safely cross an intersection. This was made even more dangerous because the intersections were narrow. The street maybe was twenty feet wide plus three feet on each side for sidewalks. If this were the case, drivers only could see twenty-six feet and beyond that they were blind. When a driver entered an intersection with a green light, he did not know if there was a driver from the other street about to run a red light. Traffic needed to creep up to the intersection, look up and down the other street, and then cross the intersection. Of course, no one did that. They took their chances. Some people slowed down for intersections, but many did not. There were many accidents.

Security on the Farm

At night, I locked all outside doors in the house, and then I locked myself inside my bedroom. In addition, I had a paid armed night watchman who walked around the outside of the house.

During the day, Don Luis was always armed.

Managua was a dangerous city, and we had the worst neighborhood in the city positioned on the east side of the farm. In this barrio, most people were unemployed, and crime was high.

Our farm had at least five acres of excellent bottomland nestled between the steep slope east of the house and the barrio. Before I arrived, the church had tried to plant crops on the bottomland, but they only had losses because most production was stolen before it was fully ripened. The church then placed a night watchman to guard the area, but I heard that he had been killed. After that, the church decided it would not use violence to protect its assets. Instead, they abandoned those acres and allowed the barrio's residences to work out a way to share the land to plant their own vegetables. That was the way the church had to turn a bad situation into a good situation. I never visited the area.

The farm had many acres of good grass, although, at that moment, it was mature and not palatable to cows. For the next year, even if the drought continued, we should have enough grass to support a few cows. I convinced the powers-to-be that we should buy a cow. Don Luis knew the perfect one. He found her somewhere and convinced her owner to part with her, and thus, we bought our first cow. She purportedly gave eight quarts of milk daily.

If we were going to have cows, we should have a way to make silage to keep them producing milk during the dry season. I convinced my supervisor to allow me to build a small horizontal silo near the building site. I needed a bricklayer, and again, Don Luis found me a bricklayer. We ordered the huge stone bricks, which were the most economic building material. I hired three brothers to help dig the opening needed on the hillside, and construction began.

I discovered quickly that the self-proclaimed bricklayer, even with the Don Luis's stamp of approval, was no guarantee of ability. I noticed that the bricks laid by our bricklayer were not straight. Evidently, our bricklayer did not know how to lay bricks. I learned that he was simply an unemployed man who would do anything to work, even misrepresent himself.

I had to find another bricklayer. I went to Don Luis and explained that we needed a real bricklayer. He could not afford to be wrong on this selection because it reflected badly on him and on me. He disappeared for a few hours and reappeared with another man carrying a toolbox with his tools. He swore he knew how to lay bricks. I asked him to show me. He started to dismantle what the previous bricklayer did and started over. I verified that he knew what he was doing and approved him to start work.

In anticipation of completing the silo, we had planted several acres of sorghum to be used to fill the silo. It was growing nicely, but we had some problems that I had never seen on our farm in Nebraska. The sorghum produced heads, which opened and started to produce seed that was easily accessible to birds. Then the parrots came. They came in mass. Great flocks of little green hungry parrots feasted on the milo heads. It was obvious that if we allowed them to continue, nothing would remain to chop for silage. We had to act.

We discussed our alternatives. We discarded having a person periodically discharge a gun because it would be too expensive. We discarded the idea of having a person periodically set off firecrackers because it would also be too expensive. The problem was that whatever we did had to be done for the twelve hours of daylight for each day until we could cut it for silage. That would consume a large volume of firecrackers or bullets. Ultimately, we agreed to hire a young boy who would carry a large biscuit can, roughly the equivalent of a five-gallon can, and a stick.

He would walk about the field and bang on the can with the stick.

This also failed because the parrots just avoided him and ate the seed-heads in another part of the field. If we hired a second boy to bang on another can, it would be too expensive. Our choice for a crop was simply not feasible in Nicaragua. We had no way to protect the seed. Even though milo was better suited to the area's climate, the bird problem made it unviable. Any future crop would have to be corn. That was the price of inexperience in the region. We were building a silo and possibly, we would have little to chop to fill the silo. I was thinking that I had taken on more than I could handle.

One day, Dr. Parajón learned how I went into town to collect the cash payroll and left it overnight under my bed. He became nervous and told me never to do that again. It was too dangerous. Neighborhood thieves had committed murder for far less cash than was stored overnight under my bed. First, he said that a different person would do the payroll every week. Second, payment would be made at a different place every week. That place would be revealed only on Saturday at noon under the shade tree at the house. It would never be far away, but still, these methods would make it more difficult for anyone to rob our payroll.

One day, while we were eating our lunch under the tablecloth, I heard three shots fired in rapid succession. The workers and I pulled our heads from under the tablecloth, dropped the tablecloth onto our plates, and looked toward the house where the sound originated. I saw Don Luis standing with his arm extended aiming for another shot. I looked toward where his pistol was pointed and saw a man running fast down the path away from the house. He was far enough away that Don Luis had no chance of hitting him. When I asked Don Luis what had happened, he told me that he had come around the corner of the house and found this man standing on the porch and looking inside the house. He thought the man was about to enter the house. That was when Don Luis shouted a warning and drew his pistol and started firing. The man quickly perceived the spot he was in and decided to vacate the premises. He may have only been looking for work.

One night we had a celebratory dinner in town and the group was taking me home after it was over. We passed onto the farm through the wire gate and arrived at the first turn where we had to turn left to reach the farmhouse. As the Land Rover made the left turn; its headlights swept across a field. In full view, we saw three men hunched over and fast walking toward the farmhouse. They appeared to be carrying machetes, but then all workers carried machetes. It could have been that they were workers from somewhere who worked late and were trying to arrive home as fast as possible, or they could have been moving toward the farmhouse with bad intentions. At that time of night, we thought the second option to be the more likely.

We quickened our pace to the farmhouse and awoke our three workers who resided in the tool shed. They dressed, grabbed their machetes, walked around the house, and then walked toward the place where we had spotted the intruders. They found no one. I was sure that the invaders had taken a different direction as soon as we had spotted them. The workers returned to their slumber. We alerted my night watchman to be on the lookout for any suspicious activity during the night and went to bed.

The three brothers finished digging the silo hole. They knew that without rain their services might no longer be needed. They asked to speak with me, and I accommodated them. They told me that, if I were to release all the workers cutting weeds, they could take over and accomplish as much as all the others. I consulted with Don Luis and he concurred.

We were far enough into what should have been the wet season, and still without enough rain to plant; we decided to abandon our idea of planting a large area to vegetables. Without the rain, it was unlikely that we could produce a crop without incurring economic losses. To minimize our losses, I would release about fifteen men who had been clearing the land of stumps and weeds. I would tell the workers on payday. I decided to retain the three brothers because they never complained, always arrived on time, and gave me a good day's work each day.

On payday, it was my turn to hand out the money. I decided to make the payment on the house porch on the farm. Most of the workers that I laid off were not surprised. They had been expecting it. Their look of despair still overwhelmed me, but I could not show it. The workers being unemployed meant, that once this money was spent, their families would experience hunger. I had already understood that I, or the church, could only help a few people for a short while--and we had already kept hunger from their doors for several weeks. We had done what we could. We were out of resources and could help them no more. Nicaragua had no relief system, no unemployment insurance, or food stamps. Every man had to provide for himself.

Some men had extended families that could help them, but these agricultural workers were in the second year of a drought. Most extended families were also drained of resources.

There was one man who, when I informed him that this was his last paycheck, had an expression that was different from the others. I noticed that he carried a fish knife in his belt. In fact, most peasant workers carried fish knives, but I never noticed them. His fish knife caught my attention because it was in plain view. I had not noticed him before, but today I noticed he had a huge scar that started at the corner of his mouth and formed an arc down his jawbone, back toward his ear, and up and around to his eye. I could only imagine that it was a fish-knife fight, and it did not look like he had won. His expression was emotionless. It caused me concern.

I paid my scar-faced worker and he disappeared. Only he reappeared an hour later, lurking about at a distance, and approached the house little by little. Don Luis saw him first.

After a few minutes, Don Luis approached the worker and asked what the worker wanted; Don

Luis smelled firewater on the worker's breath. The agitated worker demanded to speak with me. Don Luis searched for me, and when he found me, he warned me that the former worker might be confrontational. He suggested that I get on my cycle and disappear until night, to give the worker a chance to sober up. I locked the house and told Don Luis not to close the wire gate on the edge of the farm's property until I returned. He agreed. I cranked my cycle and left.

I went into town and entered an air-conditioned restaurant. I ordered, and slowly drank, two very cold Coca Colas, one after another. I then visited some friends until dark. At dark, I started back to the farm. Once I left the highway and turned onto the dirt road, I slowly rode the cycle while standing on the pegs and flashed my lights from low to high beams. My objective was to catch a reflection if a wire had been strung across the road at neck height. This was a recent method that the thieves had developed to steel motorcycles. I drove slowly, but deliberately. If I failed to see the stretched wire, it would hit my chest and do minimal damage at my low speed.

When I reached the property, the gate was supposed to be open, but it was not. This could have been a trap. Even though there were no trees on our property, there were trees, brush, and tall weeds on the other side of the fence. Any number of people could have been hiding, and I would have no clue. I had no choice but to stop, open the gate, pass through, and close it behind me. Then, I had a clear drive to the farmhouse.

On Monday morning, one of the three brothers did not appear. His name was Antonio. I asked the two remaining brothers where Antonio was. They said that he would be back on Wednesday. I asked if he was sick. No, he was not sick. I pressed for an answer. One brother finally said that he was in a little misunderstanding in a bar over the weekend and had killed someone. Now he was hiding. I asked how he was going to return to work on Wednesday with the police looking for him. They told me that, in Nicaragua, the police only look for murderers for three days. If they do not find them, the case goes cold. The police have so many new murderers to find that they cannot dwell on old cases, which are all cases four or more days old.

On Wednesday, Antonio was back and gave me a full day's work.

As I walked around the south side of Managua, there was a large prison. It had high, thick walls. On three sides there were no windows or doors, only small openings which were fewer than six by eight inches and were located high on the walls. These were probably for air circulation; however, the prisoners had another use of them. Somehow, the prisoners had managed to fabricate small containers, tie them to string and throw them up and through the openings near to high prison ceilings and lower them until they hung at street level. They just hung there until someone walked by. At this moment, the prisoners started yanking on the string and the containers came alive by moving up and down rapidly as they tried to gain the passerby's attention. The prisoners were begging for money so they could buy food to eat.

I was told that, in this prison, the prisoners were not fed. It was the prisoners' responsibility to have a family either bring them food each day or pay for prison food by any means possible. If a prisoner did not have a family that would take money, or food, to the prison, they had to find a way. Usually, this involved the prisoner finding a small paper bag and roll down the top thus forming a lip. He then tore his t-shirt or other article of clothing into strips and formed a rope. He attached the clothing rope to the paper bag with a safety pin, usually. The next hurdle was to toss the paper receptacle up and through the ventilation hole and coax the bag to drop to street level.

The sight was sad to me of all these paper cups jiggling as people walked by.

The Arrival of the Church Volunteers

One day the church bus, filled with singing passengers, arrived on the farm. When it stopped, it offloaded a bunch of young people with a smattering of middle-aged people. These were the volunteers from the church in Cleveland, Ohio. Cots had already been placed around the house to receive them. One room had cots for the female volunteers while the male volunteers were housed in my room and the kitchen area. I think we had about fifteen volunteers--and we shared one bathroom.

There were a couple of high school graduates, some college students and college graduates plus a few middle-aged teachers to help with supervising the younger volunteers. This was a happy time for me. First, I could eat with them, and their food was much better than the food that I had been eating. Second, they laughed and joked at mealtime. I admired how intelligent and quick-witted they were. Finally, there was a young female volunteer that caught my eye. I wanted to become better acquainted with her. Her name was Nancy.

The volunteers helped water plants, harvest, and package lettuce while others grabbed a hoe to help weed the growing vegetables. The lettuce was sold to the fancy hotel where Howard Hughes was thought to be staying. People were everywhere. It was hard to keep track of who was doing what, but it was nice having so many people around. It made keeping records difficult, especially for labor because the volunteers were shifting jobs at will and Julio could not keep pace with them. Also, they were not as proficient at performing tasks as the regular day laborers were.

At night, after the work was done and we ate and washed the dishes, Nancy and I would go for a walk. It was nice to have female companionship. She was a good listener and had a wonderful smile and laugh. That was the best part of my day. I had to be careful because we were always being watched by the group's elders. We made a point of always staying in view to avoid any suspicions or confrontations.

After a few days on the farm, the group was transferred to the north-coastal region of Nicaragua. It was even hotter there than in Managua. They would stay in the area's school and work with the school children.

I decided to follow their bus later the same day. The farm, without the volunteers, seemed excruciatingly quiet and intolerably boring. I could not bear it. I hit the road just after lunch and was making good time because the road was paved and mostly straight, although it did not always have much of a shoulder. If any driver needed to pull off the road for whatever reason, it would be dangerous without a wider shoulder.

I was traveling about sixty miles per hour going uphill and approaching a curve to the right. My forward vision was severely restricted by the car in front of me and the curve. That was when I noticed a truck in my side vision trying to pass me.

He was entirely in the passing lane. That was when I saw an oncoming car appear ahead of me from around the curve. The truck was only three-quarters passed me when he saw the fast-approaching car. The truck driver simply moved his truck into my lane to avoid the oncoming car. Unfortunately, I was occupying that space. I had a second to figure out what was going to happen. I tried to slow down and move to the edge of the road, even though there was no safe shoulder area. I survived and continued my journey. I had come close to a serious, and perhaps, fatal accident. All I could do was shake it off and continue down the road.

A couple of hours later I turned off the highway onto a dirt road and started to kick up some dust. Without too much trouble, I found the school, and my amigos, who were busy setting up their cots and familiarizing themselves with the outdoor toilet situation. People were selected to give each toilet a good scrubbing because they needed it. That was when the girls discovered spiders inside the toilet confines and inside the toilet. The cleaning girls came back to the group screaming. The boys charged into their toilet and bravely liquidated all visible spiders. Later, the boys did the same for the lady's toilet.

We had supper and cleaned the dishes. A group prepared a campfire. Once it had burned down a little, everyone sat around the fire, roasted marshmallows, and sang songs. I was not into singing, but I loved hearing happy people singing and joking. I loved the entire group. They were intelligent and fun to be around. Later, some of the girls asked me to check their toilet for fuzzes that might be lurking below the toilet seat. I shook out a huge spider and a lizard. Upon seeing this, some of the girls swore they would hold it in until they returned to Managua in a week or so. Others, who were more practical, marched forward and quickly did what needed to be done.

The next morning, I found my cycle's back tire flat. I had to find a small truck to carry my cycle and me into town, which was less than an hour away. After a couple of hours of waiting, I located a truck and loaded my cycle into the back of a truck, and we were off. At the tire repair station, it took an hour for them to make the repair. I paid the gentleman and started back to camp on my cycle. Halfway home my cycle started to wobble on its back tire. Yes, it was going flat again. All I could do was to push it off the road, through the deep ditch, and up on the other side, which was no small task for a heavy cycle with a flat tire. I laid it down to make it more difficult to spot from the road and buried it under dead weeds. I then applied my chain and padlock and started to walk home.

The next day I had to find another truck to take me to find my cycle, which I was worried might not be where I left it. It was. We returned to the same tire repair shop. The man found four more holes in the tire. I begged him to check every inch of the tire to avoid a repeat of the previous day. I paid and started back to camp. I worried constantly if I were going to make it, or if I would find another hole in my back tire.

The next morning, I decided that I should return to Managua to check the farm. I had become accustomed to having meals with the group filled with laughter, but I had the farm to look after.

I hit the road early, even though I was not in a hurry. I let the breeze hit my face at an easy fifty-five miles per hour. I was relaxed and enjoying the ride. Just as I passed the midway point home, I approached a small clearing on the right. It had three thatched houses with several men working around their houses. The women were either cooking or washing clothes and many children and dogs were running around. Their area was separated from the highway by a new five-barbed-wire fence. There was a gate to allow people through the fence, but not animals.

As I approached nearly even with their houses, three boys started throwing small rocks at me. One rock hit me in the solar plexus. It hurt. It was like being hit in the chest with a rock hurled at fifty-five miles per hour. I checked ahead of me and behind me. There was no traffic. I laid my cycle on its side and brought it back up on the opposite side of the road having reversed directions. I accelerated rapidly running on my back wheel and turned abruptly from the highway to the off-road next to the houses. I had their attention. The men, women, and children stopped what they were doing and focused on me, not knowing what to expect next. I revved the cycle's engine a couple times and gave a false start so that my back tire could throw sand like a dog on the beach. Now the three children started to scream and run; the fathers stood up, and I prepared to carefully guide my cycle through the narrow gate.

Once I had my cycle on their side of the fence, I accelerated behind one kid and then another. The dogs were barking while chasing me. The men began to try to reach me, but they could not. After a few seconds, I thought that I had made my point. It was time to leave. I took my cycle next to the gate, pointed my cycle sideways, idled my cycle, and shouted that the next time you throw a rock at a motorcycle; the consequences would be more serious. I turned toward the adults and shouted, "You should teach your children not to throw rocks at traffic." I passed through the gate, hit the highway, and sped away.

When I had left suddenly on my trip to follow the volunteers to their rural school, I had not made my bed. Therefore, I decided to straighten the sheets before jumping into bed. When I snapped the upper sheet, a large scorpion fell out. I secured him, took him outside, and ended his life. Upon returning to my bed, I noticed that one of my boots had fallen over. I reached down and set it upright. I heard something so I grabbed my boot, walked to the porch, and shook the boot upside down.

Out fell another large scorpion. I ended its life also. I went to bed hoping that I had not missed anymore.

The next morning, I walked around the farm to check on its status. I saw that the brick layer had finished laying the silo's floor and walls. We could now start cutting silage, even though, we had no roof. Don Luis was sent to find a corn chopper and a motor to power it. He came back with a nice chopper, but the motor was old, and I mean old, motor. I was not convinced that it would even run. Don Luis grabbed a rope and with one try, the motor grunted into action. It sounded like our old John Deere Model A tractor. It gave a puff of life, and then made me wonder if it had died before another puff of life appeared. It took a few cycles of puffs and no puffs before I was confident that it was working.

We had a couple of men in the milo field cutting the milo stalks at their base. We had also hired a pair of oxen and an ox cart to haul the sorghum stalks from the field to the silo. Once at the silo, the stalks were unloaded while one man eased a few stalks at a time into the silage cutter. The motor just kept grunting and groaning and the cutter kept on cutting. The milo heads had only a smattering of seeds, but we had to take it the way it came from the field.

Seeing that our milo would not be enough to fill the silo, we bought the neighbor's corn field. It had good stalks of corn with respectably large ears, but unfortunately, the stand was very thin. We also took what came from the field. By this time, we had a barrel filled with water that was pushed up and down the silage in the silo to compact it and drive out as much oxygen as possible. As we finished cutting the silage, the roof was being placed on the silo. We were now ready for the dry season, even if we had not had a wet season.

After a week, the church group returned to the farm and spread out to view how the farm had changed during the last few days. There was again chatter and laughter around the farmhouse. That evening, I took Nancy for a walk around the farm to show her what had been done and explained to her why it had been done. On a usual day on the farm, I spoke little and then, only to farm hands. It became very monotonous and uninteresting.

The next evening, I obtained permission to take Nancy for a motorcycle ride to Lake Managua. We left early evening. I parked the cycle on the edge of the path that vehicles take to the lake. We had to walk an additional fifty yards or so to the water's edge. The shore was dirt and not sand, as I had imagined it. We talked. I was sad because I knew she would be returning to start her freshman year in nursing at the University of Vermont in a few days. I would be very alone after the group left. I had become accustomed to their company.

As we talked and walked along the shoreline, I caught a glance of movement near my cycle. I saw one National Guardsman walking around my cycle and examining it closely. I saw a second Guardsman positioning himself in a shadow under a streetlight. This was not good. There had been many cases of bad behavior by Guardsmen when a lone female was involved. I did not like what I saw. I made an excuse that we needed to return to the farmhouse, while I placed my hand in the middle of her back and turned her in the opposite direction; we started walking toward the motorcycle, slowly. I pointed out to her the presence of the Guardsmen. I told her to mount the cycle as soon as she arrived. I started a conversation with the Guardsmen near the cycle. He was asking me questions. I answered them, but I continued to mount the cycle and started it. I put it in gear and left him talking to the air. I had no idea if they had had bad intentions toward my cycle, or toward Nancy, but we successfully left them behind and returned to the farmhouse. I never told Nancy about my worries.

The time came for the group to leave. I was crushed by the silence and sadness on the farm without them. Even the farm workers seemed saddened by their absence.

As time passed, I had sunk into a depression that only seemed to become worse with time. I missed Nancy. My work on the farm gave me less and less satisfaction. I started to consider leaving Nicaragua. Before I could leave, I needed to look for my replacement. I went to the Peace Corps office and learned that an agricultural volunteer had just enlisted for a third year in Nicaragua. I convinced him and the Peace Corps to allow him to take over for me. I informed my supervisor of my impending departure. I explained that I had found someone to take on the task of managing the farm. They were sad to see me leave but happy that I had found someone to carry on my work.

I sold my motorcycle to a Mennonite agricultural volunteer. I would miss my beautiful motorcycle. I bought an airline ticket to Burlington, Vermont, and said my goodbyes. I was excited because I had never been east of the Missouri River.

I arrived in Burlington at night, a chilly Vermont night. Nancy picked me up and took me to her dormitory. I needed a day or two to find my own place and a few more to find a job. It was a little clumsy at the dormitory, but none of her colleagues seemed shocked to see a man in their dormitory. Much had changed since I had graduated from the University of Nebraska just a couple of years previous, or perhaps the change was not due to time but regional. Vermont was much worldlier due to so many students arriving from New York City, Boston, and other large urban areas.

I found a room that I rented by the day. It was tiny but adequate. My main problem was transportation. I could not find work without a car. Within days, I was able to buy a Volkswagen Beatle. This would be excellent for the deep snow that would be coming soon. In fact, it was already cold. I needed to buy winter clothes. My clothes were appropriate only for the Nicaraguan heat.

Once I had a room, a car, and clothes, I looked for a job. I found a part-time job in the Natural Resources department at the University of Vermont. I worked for a Mormon professor of economics. I enjoyed my job. Mostly, I was an errand boy, but that was fine. At lunchtime, the professor would kick back in his chair and talk to me about economics. He was conservative, but his logic was impeccable. It was working for him where I learned how important it was to understand statistics.

I wanted to move out of my room and into an apartment, but I did not make enough money for that. I started seeking a second part-time job. I found one at a gas station. I now worked thirty hours a week at the university and thirty hours a week at the gas station. I rented a nice small apartment in a neighboring town where rent was cheaper than in the university town of Burlington.

I was busy. I did my laundry and my shopping on Saturdays plus I worked at the gas station. On Sundays, I only worked at the gas station. That was when I cooked a hot meal that included baked ham, sweet potatoes, and green beans. I always looked forward to that. It was the only hot meal I had during the week. Each morning, I made six ham sandwiches, because I would eat lunch at the university and eat supper while on duty at the gas station. I would arrive home at 10:00 p.m. most nights.

On December 23rd, 1972, while I was working at the gas station, a special news edition appeared on the radio announcing that, earlier that morning, a strong earthquake had rocked Nicaragua, centered on Managua. I was dumbfounded. As I listened to more details from the radio announcement, I wondered about each of my friends living there. I tried to envision the status of their homes and apartments. I knew that Dr. Parajón would be busy caring for those injured by the earthquake, but I wondered about what the others would be doing, but most of all, I worried about if they were safe.

Between customers, I went to a place behind the front desk, sat, held my head in my hands, and tried to understand the gravity of what had happened. I confess that tears formed, and I had to brush them aside, especially when the outside bell rang informing me that a new customer had arrived at the gas station.

The next few days were no better. I received more and more news from the radio and television stations, but I had no specific news about my friends. I don't remember the estimates of the day as to how many people were killed, injured, or left homeless, but it would have been very high numbers. Today, I checked Wikipedia and they estimated that from 4,000 to 11,000 people were killed, 20,000 were injured and 300,000 were left homeless out of a total population of one million.

I wrote a letter to Joan Parajón, the American wife of Dr. Parajón. I had no idea if the letter would ever reach her, given the mess that the earthquake had left Managua in. After a few weeks, I received a letter from Joan bringing me up to date on my friends. They were all unhurt. Finally, I could relax. I resolved to visit Nicaragua at the end of the semester and see for myself what had happened.

Meanwhile, my Mormon supervisor recommended that in January I start to take economics courses. I took his advice and took two courses: farm management and production economics, but I kept working sixty hours a week. I never had a spare moment, but I liked my life. I was learning useful skills and making money.

As my university supervisor became better acquainted with my personality, he recommended that I take courses in the economics department, plus courses in calculus and statistics. Of course, being hard-headed, I rejected his recommendations. I had found my introductory courses in economics very boring and did not want to take more of the same. He then guided me to another department on campus--a new department. I enrolled for a master's degree in Adult Education and prepared for my trip to Nicaragua.

Once again, Juan met me at the airport and took me to Dr. Parajon's house. I was very emotional because we had to drive a detour around Managua to reach the house. Where Managua had once been a busy city, it now had a four barbed wire fence around it and only a few buildings stood. Joan told me that she had told another friend, Jimmy, an American church volunteer, that I was coming. He had managed to rent a newly constructed temporary house in recent development and welcomed me to stay with him while I was in Managua.

Juan drove me there and showed me the place. Jimmy was at work. It was a very adequate one-bedroom apartment with a living room large enough to have a second bedroom available for his many guests. It seems Jimmy was the go-to guy to house guests when someone from outside Nicaragua flew in for some reason. Later, I saw Jimmy and it seemed like yesterday that we had last seen each other, yet it seemed like ten years because of all that had happened.

The next day I received a ride to the fence placed around the destroyed center of Managua and took my camera. I carefully swung my legs between two barbed wires and started walking where Managua had once been a vibrant city. These were the streets where I had ridden my motorcycle on the weekends to get away from the farm. The streets had been full of cars, trucks, motorcycles, and people. It was hard to go far without stopping for someone or something that was in my way. And now, I saw a lone stalk of corn growing in the once busiest of streets.

Not a person or car could be seen in any direction.

I looked up at a tall building, perhaps fifteen stories. During the quake, the first story had collapsed, as it had in many buildings, but on top of this building was a man with a sledgehammer standing on the outside wall chipping away at the structure. Why was he there? What did he hope to accomplish? He had to be the most optimistic man in the world to be chipping away at such a large building, but there he was.

After a week of finding and meeting with my old friends, I felt better. I could breathe again. I said my goodbyes and returned to Vermont.

My time at the University of Vermont had achieved one major thing; it awoke my desire to learn. It gave me a taste of learning useful skills from my classes in agricultural economics, especially farm management. I had a new respect for university learning and looked forward to using all my non-major credit hours on taking the few agricultural economics courses taught in the Department of Natural Resources.

I spent the next year taking my courses, working, and trying to have a social life. I graduated and left the university for my second Peace Corps tour, this time in Brazil—but that is another story.

Short-Term Volunteer Assignments in Nicaragua

After I had lived an adventure-filled ten years in Brazil followed by twenty-five years without adventure working at normal jobs in the US, I needed another adventure. One day, while doing research on the internet, I discovered the existence of short-term volunteer assignments in other countries. These trips were paid for by the U.S. government. They awarded contracts to nongovernment organizations (NGO's) to supervise projects that involved specific countries and tasks to be completed in each country. Each assignment lasted between ten and twenty-one days, depending on the country. If the country were in Africa, Eastern Europe, or Asia, the assignment would call for eighteen to twenty-one days due to the enormous transportation expense. If it were located closer, like Nicaragua, it could be as brief as ten days.

I found that I could work these trips in between semester breaks. I signed up for assignments in the Caribbean area and Nicaragua. It didn't take long for a trip to Nicaragua to materialize.

Trip 1—The Eco-lodge—May 4, 2012

I arose at 3:00 a.m. to make my flight. I arrived at the airport in good time; however, I was surprised by the already long lines. They moved slowly, but, even so, I made my flight to Miami. The good part was that I did not have to wait for boarding. The plane was full, and the seats were small, or perhaps I was too large for the seats.

The flight was short, just over two hours. The time spent in Miami was agreeable. I had time to eat a large slice of reheated pizza.

The flight to Managua was nearly empty. The plane had a capacity for 180 people, and we were only twenty-five on board. I dozed most of the way. Before I could become tired from the flight, we were descending into Managua. I was anxious to see what Managua looked like after an absence of forty years.

De-boarding was almost immediate, as was passing through customs and collecting the baggage. I went outside to wait for my people to find me. It was humid and hot, about ninety-five degrees. Within minutes I was greeting by Elisa and Fernando. They were both very personable. We reentered the airport for them to eat a quick sandwich. The pizza still filled my stomach. We talked as they ate, but I found my forty-year-old Spanish a little rusty. I spoke ninety percent

Portuguese with it; although, they understood. They both exuded competence and excitement.

As we loaded the pickup, a covered Ford 150, they informed me that we were headed into the rural area directly from the airport and would spend the first week at an agricultural high school. From Managua, we headed northeast towards Matagalpa. The road was recently repaved and uncommonly smooth. We were not always making good time because of the traffic. There were many heavily loaded trucks, which struggled to carry their load uphill. It was a constant uphill grade as we proceeded toward Matagalpa. Elisa drove carefully and we often found ourselves behind slow-moving trucks.

In Matagalpa, we stopped at a local farm coop to purchase eight sacks of seed that they would need later. The city of Matagalpa had 400 plus thousand inhabitants but consisted of narrow streets and regular adobe brick houses.

As we left Matagalpa, Fernando took the wheel. We made a couple of other quick stops and then we continued toward our destination, Jinatega. The sign indicated that it was thirty-two kilometers away, about twenty miles.

We climbed ever higher. The grade increased and the average speed decreased. We were surrounded by mountains and valleys filled with forests and coffee plantations. There were many coffee processing plants along the side of the road. Nestled in the small areas of relatively flat good soil were small areas of vegetable production. Bananas and plantain were also scattered about. At one place, above our road, I saw a herd of cattle grazing on a pasture so steep that, if one cow should lose its footing, it would have rolled a mile downhill before it stopped.

The roadsides were laced with many natural growing flowers. We saw greenhouses where flowers were grown commercially. They offered opportunities to buy them at the roadside. The road grew narrower and the new pavement disappeared. In its place was a road filled with rocks that caused the truck to bounce and potholes that added to the discomfort. Our average speed decreased even more as Fernando tried to maneuver around the rocks and potholes. Darkness was fast approaching. We saw a huge lake located in a valley that did not show on the map. It was gorgeous. I wanted to stop to take photographs, but we still had far to go.

We asked for directions a couple of times. The road became ever narrower and, unbelievably, with more and deeper potholes and more uneven rocks. We often did not pass five or ten miles per hour. Finally, we came to the point where we turned to the right. The road was instantly less traveled and now, was only the width of the truck. It was now dark. I don't mean US-city-dark. I mean rural-dark in a country with no rural electrification. I mean you could see nothing beyond the vehicle's headlights. In addition, I was now hungry and exhausted.

Finally, we came to a small bridge. It had a bypass road that took us down a steep slope, across a stream, and up on the other side. We guessed that the bypass was to be used for trucks too heavy for the wooden bridge. Then there was the bridge. We stopped. Fernando and Elisa viewed the bridge from all angles and discussed it. Would the wooden planks support the pickup? They opted for the bridge. I silently disagreed. I did not trust the bridge. Its planks did not inspire confidence. My heart stopped and my hands clutched my things tightly. And then we were over it. I breathed again. I was so happy that it was behind me until the next one appeared. It was the same as before. They viewed and discussed it and agreed to give the bridge a try. My heart stopped, but we made it. When the third bridge appeared, I was already a pro and had more faith in the bridge. There was a fifth and sixth bridge and, finally, there was no bridge and we had to go through the water. We were now at the end of a six-month dry season and the water was moving fast and was a foot deep. I cannot imagine doing this during the rainy season.

We stopped more to ask for directions. We were told that we were on the right path. As our truck struggled to move up the steep slopes, we saw a sign that warned drivers to stop and engage the four-wheel-drive before attempting the remaining slope. Fernando heeded the warning and placed the truck in low gear and floored the accelerator. The truck was spinning its wheels and bouncing as it forced its way up the last hill.

We parked the truck. I thought that whoever selected this site had an interesting sense of humor. In Brazil, we would say that this is where the wind goes before it turns around to come back.

This was the Eco-Lodge where we would stay. It generated all its own electricity via solar panels and stored the energy in batteries. We unpacked and were shown our rooms. I had a beautiful room with a bathroom. Even though the light bulb was weak, I could see to unpack; there was not enough light to read. I returned to the main patio because it was a roofed area without walls. We began talking and ordered food. It was simple food, but delicious. I ate beans, scrambled eggs with ham and cheese. All food had been produced on the area's agricultural high school property. It was delicious. After eating, we had our coffee and to bed, I went. My day had already been extremely long.

May 6, 2012—The Long Walk

It was 4:00 p.m. Sunday. I was sitting on the back porch of my cottage. The ground was twenty feet down. I was looking into a mountain that was higher than my position. I did not care to guess how much higher, but I had no desire to hike to its summit. It was a rain forest, but under the canopy was a coffee plantation. The same mountain curved around to my right. To my left, was a descent into a valley. Birds were chirping and a few crickets were active. I was sitting in a rocking chair made of wood similar to mahogany. My best guess was that it weighed forty pounds. The wood was thick and heavy. Earlier, I tried to move a small table and almost pulled my back. It was smaller than a card table and likely weighed sixty pounds. The wooden top was more than one and a half inches thick and the brace boards were three-quarters of an inch thick.

I am the only person in the eco-lodge, other than a cook left here to attend to my needs. There was nothing to do. I had been preparing for tomorrow's lecture at the agricultural high school, but I did not know what to talk about. This area was so different from anything I had seen.

This eco-lodge consisted of eight apartments with two places for camping with a tent. Each cabin consisted of two apartments. The school and the lodge were self-contained. All electricity was solar-generated. Each apartment had a weak light in the bedroom and another in the bathroom. It was sufficient to see to pack, unpack, select clothes, but never to read. For that, we needed to open the doors or the window and allow the sun to pour in during the day. At night, there was no possibility of reading. The hot water was also heated by solar energy. It was more practical to take a shower in the late afternoon than in the morning. An early morning shower could be disagreeable due to cool water. By late afternoon, the sun had had time to work its magic on the water by warming it to an agreeable temperature.

Yesterday was a day that I will not soon forget. I awoke before 7:00 a.m. After discovering the problem with taking a hot shower, I washed quickly, dressed, and descended to the kitchen. I ate a breakfast consisting of rice and black beans, French bread, and two eggs. Soon, my colleagues had arrived and had also eaten. I was told that we had a meeting with the person in charge of the project. I envisioned a meeting in an office and then off to another site in our truck. I placed my camera in the truck seat. I was told that the young high school girl who served as our waitress would accompany us. I had no idea why. She was sixteen years old and was a second-year student in high school. She was studying hotel management.

We stood around for a few minutes waiting. The waitress, Hazel, was preparing the receipt for a young American couple.

They were checking out of the lodge. Elisa suddenly motioned for us to follow her. I did. We started down the same road we had climbed the night before. It was very steep. I had to carefully place each step to ensure that I did not fall. I could not take a step more than six to eight inches without risking sliding on the loose rocks. Soon, I began to think we were not going to return to the pickup. It was then she noticed that I had not taken my camera. She told us to wait for her and she started back up the road to fetch my camera. We waited forty minutes before she reappeared with Hazel, the couple who had checked out, and my camera. Now I was confused, but I said nothing.

We proceeded down the mountain until we reached the school. It was there that Hazel started to show us the school and explain every detail. Now, I understood. She was going to give us a tour of the school. After several minutes, Elisa explained to me that she and Fernando were taking the truck and leaving. They would return next Thursday to retrieve me. I was to continue the tour with Hazel. They told me that on Monday, I would address the school and give them a lecture on pasture management, intensive grazing and show them how to build and maintain an electric fence. And they left. I didn't have time to tell them that I had never erected a high-tensile fence. I had watched once while a contractor installed such a fence in a large pasture.

By now, it was hot, and I sipped slowly on my half-gallon of water that I was carrying with me. From the school, we continued downhill. We turned and visited a small garden patch and then continued downhill, and then uphill. It was a steep hill, a very steep hill. I was quickly gasping for air. We were on our way to see the school's hog facilities. After a thorough tour of the facility, we retraced our steps to the main road, where Hazel turned away from the school. Her comment was, "and now we walk awhile before our next stop." I did not see this as encouraging. It was hot. I was sweating profusely, sipping on my water and my feet were hurting. I was trying to ration my water because I had no idea how long it had to last.

We passed huge trees. It was difficult to judge their height, but 100 feet was probably within reason with their circumferences being between fifteen and twenty-five feet. We walked uphill and then downhill again. We started crossing the bridges that we had crossed the night before, first one, then two, and then several. I noticed that most had been safe; however, I saw one that was questionable. If our tire had moved a couple feet to one side, the plank would not likely have supported our vehicle's weight. But that could be my imagination because many trucks used the bridge daily and no one (that I knew of) had fallen.

Eventually, we arrived at the place where they maintained their chickens and cattle. We saw the chickens. The place smelled like our old chicken house on the farm. They maintained three hundred laying hens. Most of the production was consumed at the agricultural school and the eco-lodge. All surplus production was sold in town and the money was used to buy supplies for the school and the lodge.

We went toward the cattle. Hazel started climbing up the pasture. This was not a horizontal pasture. It was a vertical pasture. It was at least on a forty-five-degree slope, or so it seemed. I think the cows must have taken a course in mountain climbing before being released into such a pasture. It was time for the rains to begin, but they had not arrived, so the pasture was very dry. At least fifty percent of the land was bare, and the rest had no grass more than one inch tall. It had been severely over-grazed. I saw several cows climbing the slope, as did Hazel, all without difficulty. I could only take a couple steps without resting. I continued to sweat profusely. My feet hurt from walking on slopes and on rocks. I looked at my watch. It was exactly noon when I drank the last of my water. There was no need to ration it. I needed it.

We started back. I did not know how I was going to make it. The young Americans and

Hazel glided along like the young people they were. I did not glide. I often had to rest. They, considerately, waited for me to resume. Our progress was slow. When we had relatively flat walking, I tried to walk as fast as I could so as not to hold them back, but I still could not match their pace.

Soon, the young Americans' taxi arrived from the city to pick them up and they left us to travel in the opposite direction. Now, it was Hazel and me. I truly had never been so tired, so exhausted, and as unsure as to how I would complete the journey. Finally, at 2:00 p.m. we reached the school again. Hazel took my bottle to fill it with water. I sat in the shade. I peeled my camera from my body, my glasses, my wristwatch, and anything else that I could. It was then I noticed that my hands were swollen. My fingers were so large that I could not make a fist. When I extended them, the tips of my fingers did not touch because they were so thick at the base.

She appeared with the water. Within five minutes I had emptied the half-gallon container. She re-filled it. I rested for about thirty minutes before continuing. After a couple hundred yards up the mountain, she suggested we take a shortcut. I thought that anything would be better than trying to climb over the loose rocks that filled the road. She turned into the woods with coffee plants all around us. The path was dirt and was about two to three feet wide. To make the path, they had carved out dirt two to three feet deep. The mountain was very steep. Taking a misstep would guarantee a long fall before the coffee trees could stop our descent. The path wound back and forth, but it generally had a gentle slope compared to the road. I still had to rest, but I knew I was going to make it.

Finally, there it was--the eco-lodge. It was 3:00 p.m. I dragged myself to my cabin and jumped into the best shower of my life. It felt so good. I washed the sweat from my hair and beard and rinsed. Then, I lay in my bed and rested. I thought I would never again move; however, after an hour my stomach was begging me for food. Eventually, my stomach won.

After eating, it was 5:00 p.m. and perfectly light. I discovered my back porch and sat in the rocking chair and stared at the mountains. The crickets were singing, and birds were chirping. I noticed that dusk was descending very slowly. I was confused because my memory of dusk in El Salvador and Nicaragua was that, within twenty minutes, it went from bright light to dusk and then into total darkness. I did not recall a gentle transition as I was now experiencing. As dusk overcame the late afternoon brightness, more crickets joined in their singing and they sang even louder. Then there's the frog; I decided to call him Fred, the Frog and he started his song. I believe him to be a bachelor looking for his soul mate, but never finding it. He sang and sang and then, perhaps, he slept. Anyway, his singing stopped.

During the night, the noise was mostly crickets and birds. Occasionally, I heard nothing.

May 7, 2012 – The Agricultural High School

On this day, I was to make a presentation to the high school students. They had a modern classroom with a computer, an overhead projector, and a sturdy white screen. I gave my presentation. I spoke slowly, hoping that the students would understand what I said. One instructor asked many questions, which I believed added to the students' understanding. The students did not seem to be interested—they were too young to appreciate the details they were being given.

In the afternoon we visited a plantation of tall grass that could be cut into silage. We took a balance with us to weigh the material. I measured off several small and equal areas and had a student cut and separate the grass from each area. Each area's grass was weighed and recorded. This exercise was to ensure they knew how to properly cut and weigh grass. Later, they would cut and weigh the grass as an experiment to determine the optimal time intervals to cut grass on the entire production area.

The homework I left them was to return in two weeks and cut the first small area and weigh the result. After one more week, cut the second plot and weigh. After each additional week, cut and weigh the results from each additional plot. The instructor would then make the necessary adjustments and determine what the optimal time should be between cuttings to maximize the production from this small, planted area of tall grass. Done properly, they could increase their grass and silage production considerably.

The next day I packed and made my return trip to Managua, filled out my final report, and returned home.

Trip 2—Managua, Nicaragua—October 2015

On this assignment, I was to assist a new nationwide project to improve beef production. The country was divided into several regions and each region was to receive its own beef production specialist. It would operate like my time with Farmers National Company and the management of farms. I had about sixty farms to manage and I had to visit each farm every five weeks. Each visit had a series of tasks that I had to complete, such as sign the lease, determine the crop production plan, monitor soil conservation structures, and a host of other items. The beef production specialists had to periodically visit each ranch and complete specific tasks with the rancher. These results had to be documented and periodically sent to their national headquarters.

The national committee had prepared booklets that would be used for each rancher.

Results would be entered on the appropriate page in the appropriate booklet and saved. Periodically, they would be entered into Excel spreadsheets where these files would be sent to the national office in Managua and consolidated into a national data bank for analysis and research. My job was to create the Excel spreadsheets for each beef production specialist to fill in and then send them to Managua for evaluation, summarization, and storage for future studies.

October 21, 2015—Visiting Farms

I just returned from five days in Matagalpa. Matagalpa is a city of 400,000 people nestled in the mountains (really foothills) in northern Nicaragua. We did not stay in the city but in a hostel located above the city. Our elevation was almost 4,000 feet, which made sleeping enjoyable. It was a big modern house with the owner also cooking for us. She acted like a mother away from home. She had a big dog that was always sneaking into the house and either lying on the floor by us or encouraging us to pet her. The owner never wanted her in the house because she smelled a little, but the dog was very sneaky and we, of course, helped her hide.

Our trip from Managua to Matagalpa on Friday late afternoon took three hours to cover eighty miles. In addition to the normal dangers of car travel in Nicaragua, we had Friday after work travel, plus it started to rain. Eventually, it rained heavily. I did not know how our driver kept us safe. He drove very slowly, and, in such times, patience is a virtue.

The first day we visited a 160-acre ranch, which was located ten miles northeast of Matagalpa. The road was always uphill, so its elevation was high. The ranch was very well run by a son (agricultural degree from the U.S.) and his father. Their farm was divided into halves with half the grass being planted to improved grass and the other half remaining in native pasture. It had a river running through it and had steep slopes leading from the mountains into the river and large and tall trees. It was a beautiful farm.

They had about thirty milk cows. They currently sold the milk in the local town, but they were building a state-of-the-art cheese-making area where they intended to produce cheese. For machinery, they had a thirty-horsepower tractor that they used to pull a small wagon with whatever needed to be pulled, and a larger truck that they used to bring a by-product from the beer brewery in Managua. This was used as a supplemental feed for the cows. They did not buy any concentrate because it was much too expensive.

The father and son both lived in Matagalpa, but the father had built a nice one-bedroom house on the farm. He stayed there during his daily visits to the farm, sometimes staying overnight.

On Sunday, we visited another farm located much higher in the mountains. It was owned by a family that was half German and half Nicaraguan. The organization on the farm was German. It was highly organized, and everything was in its place. They operated a very high-end hotel located above the farm. They produced almost everything that was eaten at the hotel. They had milk cows that produced milk and calves. The calves, when grown, supplied meat and replacements for their milk cows. They had chickens producing eggs and broilers, and they had pigs. The leftovers from cheese making were fed to the pigs. The chicken poop was fed to the milk cows for protein. The cow poop and pig poop went into a bio-digester which produced gas that was used for cooking at the farm laborers' houses. They also produced coffee, bananas, plantain, oranges, and other stuff.

I worked on developing Excel spreadsheets for receiving the data from the calf project, which should allow sophisticated reports to be drawn from it. This was very intense work. My bottom could not tolerate chairs anymore and the muscles in my hands, arms, and neck were stiff, but I must continue. I needed to make a presentation to the bosses in Managua on Friday afternoon.

October 22, 2015—Background on my Nicaraguan Counterparts

I continued my work on the Excel model, but I was still gaining insight into what they needed. This trip was only the tip of the iceberg for what they really needed. They needed an experienced systems analyst and programmer. What they had (me) was much less than that, but I could get them started.

A few minutes ago, as I was eating lunch, and a horse with a cart passed by in the street. That reminded me that when I was here in 1972, there were many horses and carts in the streets and even many oxen pulling carts. I had not seen one pair of oxen pulling a cart and only a very few horses pulling carts this trip. That must imply that economic development has occurred in the intervening forty years.

The professionals I had been working with were fifty to sixty years old now. From 1975 to 1979 (approximately) there was a civil war in Nicaragua. That was thirty-five to forty years ago. These professionals were from fifteen to twenty-five years old during the civil war. Most were drafted into the government's army to fight. One was awarded a scholarship to study veterinary medicine in Moldova (Eastern Europe) and, later, a master's degree in Brazil in agricultural economics. He spoke Spanish, Russian, and Portuguese fluently and can conduct a basic conversation in English. He spoke to me of the structured and rigorous education that he received while in Moldova. He had to work hard and always stayed focused. He had little time for recreation.

If my memory serves me correctly, in 1979 Somoza was forced to leave the country, which was good. The Somoza family had been exploiting the Nicaraguan people for fifty-five years. It was time for him to leave. Our U.S. government gave its full support to this vicious man and helped him stay in power.

Once the government was established to replace Somoza, the new Nicaragua government closed all high schools and universities for one year. The students were scattered around

Nicaragua to teach literacy skills to the poor people who had been denied education under Somoza. Each student lived with a local family and ate what the family ate. In many cases that was little more than lumps of sugar derived from their own sugar cane production. The students received no financial support from the government and most families were unable to help. These students learned much about how difficult a peasant's life was. It was burned into their brain. During this time, the students noticeably raised the proportion of the Nicaraguan population that was now literate. This process changed how the students perceived the world.

Those who had been drafted into the army learned discipline and organization. Currently, the professionals in this age group are focused, determined, hardworking, and remember the difficulties the peasants confronted while they, as students, lived with the peasants. They are determined to improve the quality of life for all segments of the population. I am impressed with the new Nicaragua that I found compared to the one I saw in 1972.

At 6:30 p.m. I was invited to have dinner with friends that I made in 1972. They lived on the other side of town. Their house does not have a specific address. I hoped I could find it. I did not have a workable cell phone. Another worry was how I would return after dinner. It may be difficult to find a taxi. Since none of the streets in my area have names, I must tell the taxi driver to turn left for x blocks and then right for y blocks and they may not be able to follow my directions. I hope my instructions will be correct. Without a phone and a specific address, it was difficult to navigate from one place to another.

October 23, 2015—A Country Meeting

The reunion with my friends was perfect. I found their house, had a nice meal with an even better conversation, and my taxi came to pick me up on time.

For the next part of my assignment, I visited a dairy farm where many neighboring beef and dairy producers were to gather in the farm's dairy barn. The barn only had walls that were four feet high. The roof had two layers with vertical space between them to allow hot air to escape upward and add to the ventilation. I was designated to give a talk on the advantages of cross-fencing and the use of high tensile fencing.

We arrived early before anyone else had arrived. Soon, other presenters arrived and started setting up a computer that was connected to show slides on a white sheet that had been placed in one corner of the barn. I knew this was unlikely to work since there was a significant breeze that was blowing the sheet in all directions. This made it difficult for us to view any kind of stable imagine.

Outside one partial wall, in the shade of the barn, was a feeder filled with freshly cut grass. The cows were fighting for the best positions in the trough. It was an easy way to determine which cows were dominant in the herd. Whoever was addressing the crowd had to speak louder than the cows fighting over silage.

Over the next hour, several dozen people arrived and started to seek each other out and talk about cows, fences, and pastures. The other presenters were still trying to find a way to stabilize the white sheet but without much success. They tied the corners, but the center of the sheet moved in and out and then to the side. I started thinking about changing my presentation so that the computer would not be needed.

There were two ladies in the corner of the barn B-B-Qing and preparing lunch for all guests and presenters. Finally, they opened the meeting. People quieted and found a chair to sit on. The president of the beef and dairy producers gave a brief statement and introduced the first presenter. All the presenters struggled with the dancing white sheet, but the attendees pretended that they were seeing the slides as they were intended to be seen.

Finally, it was my turn. I explained the advantages of dividing large pastures into smaller paddocks. I explained how many paddocks they should have, at least ideally. I explained how the types of grass in each paddock were important. They needed to conduct an inventory of grasses across the larger pasture and use the results to delineate the smaller pastures by keeping the grasses as homogeneous as possible within each paddock. I explained how water should be distributed and how the fencing should be done and how often they should move the cattle from one paddock to another. I used no slides. I stood in the center of the attendees and spoke as loudly as I could. The cows and calves offered competition for our attendees' ears.

Afterwards, lunch was served, and people grabbed the food and ate. Only after eating did they stand and approach each presenter to ask further questions. I felt it had been a very productive afternoon. I also wondered what my university students would think if they had seen me deliver a lecture in Spanish in an open-air dairy barn without the benefit of any teaching aide.

October 24, 2015—The Agricultural University

There was also a day at the region's agricultural university where specialists in pasture management and beef and dairy management had been invited to make presentations to the university's students. I had been invited to make the same presentation that I had made to the beef and dairy producers; only this time the university had a proper computer and overhead projector with a stable screen.

Even with a microphone, I had to speak very slowly and loudly, hoping that the students would understand my imperfect Spanish. I made my presentation using my slides as best as I could. As soon as we could, we left because we still had a long drive to make.

It was late afternoon and I had not eaten since that morning's light breakfast. I was starved and had a throbbing headache because of it. Finally, after almost three hours of driving, we found a restaurant and I ate ravenously.

The next day, the Dean of the College of Agriculture invited me to attend his graduate class in statistics. The classrooms were not air-conditioned and were hot, just as hot as it was outside, or hotter. There were two classrooms back-to-back separated only by a collapsing wall. The other classroom was also occupied with students attending another lecture. They maintained the wall half-open; I suppose to enhance air circulation. Students had to focus on their lecturer because of the constant interference from the neighboring classroom.

Suddenly, the Dean invited me to give a short lecture on any topic I chose. This was not in any plans that we had made. I decided to show them how I used the coefficient of variation to make important decisions in agriculture. I used it to decide whether to renew a farm lease with a farmer. I used it to determine what the best crop rotation was for a specific farm. I emphasized that; although it was a simple concept, it had great value in making agricultural decisions.

After lunch, they returned me to my hotel. My work was done. I returned to my hotel room and finished my report to the NGO and handed it in. Early the next day I returned to the USA.

In-country Interview for a Job in Romania – January 1999

I had a market research job in St. Louis that I hated. The job was fine. It was the people I did not like. I was looking around quietly for another job.

For months I had been following an announcement by a company for a job in Romania. They had been advertising it and then delayed it for unknown reasons. I thought the job had disappeared when it reappeared suddenly. I obtained an interview by telephone, which I thought went well. A few days later, the company invited me to a second interview—in Romania. I was ecstatic. I had never been to Europe or Eastern Europe. I started making my preparations for the trip. I even paid extra to have my passport fast-tracked. My wife was not happy, but I was dying for some adventure in my life. It had been twelve years since I had moved back from Brazil. I needed a new adventure to keep me going. I also thought that I could make some good money because it looked like my skills would be perfect for this job and overseas jobs usually paid very well.

The project I would be working on, as I understood it, was a complicated one that would have a five-year life. An American entrepreneur had created this agricultural project that would involve the Romanian government (2% stake), hundreds of small farmers (47% stake), and himself (51% stake). To earn their two percent stake, the Romanian government would supervise their vast irrigation pumps and water distribution systems. They had the largest water pumps in the world. They pumped water from the Danube River. For the small farmers' stake, they would provide the labor to make the project work. The American entrepreneur would finance the project, provide modern machines and equipment and material (seed, fertilizer, and chemicals), and would market all the corn produced. The land and labor in Romania had been unutilized since the decline of the Soviet Union.

I was not sure what my exact duties would be, but I was sure it would be exciting.

I packed my suitcase and could not contain my excitement. My wife, however, did not share my enthusiasm because she did not see any advantages to this job. She was more worried about what this separation would do to our marriage. I was selfish and had not even thought about that. I simply needed an adventure. I was dying. I needed to learn a new language and accumulate new stories to tell. I was looking for another Peace Corps adventure but with much higher income potential. I had not fully understood how this being a private, commercial enterprise might change any experiences that I would have. At best, it was a half-baked idea, but one that gave me a needed shot of adrenaline when I was very unhappy with my life.

The day arrived to depart. I do not remember the cities through which I passed, but there were many. My host was saving as much money as possible by buying the cheapest flights, but I didn't mind because I would soon be able to claim that I had been to Europe and Eastern Europe.   I arrived in Bucharest, the capital of Romania, in the dark of night. Being January, it was cold and dreary. Almost no one was in the streets. I was collected at the airport by a driver and taken down narrow streets that contained the remnants of snow-covered with a black layer of coal dust or some other pollutant. Eventually, the driver stopped in front of a nondescript house, out of a line of houses that could have been in Latin America if it had not been for the cold and the black snow. The driver knocked on the door and, after a minute, someone came to the door, welcomed me, motioned for me to grab my luggage and follow him. He led me to a tiny bedroom in what was a tiny apartment.

The next morning, I was offered a simple breakfast and rushed off across the city to a simple office. There I met seven other job candidates. Surprise! I thought I was the only candidate. The project manager was also present. The project manager explained that there were six positions and eight candidates. He went on to explain that we would visit some of the existing land sites for the project and spend a week in daily meetings with former collective farms that were applying for the honor to participate in the project.

The project manager explained that the old Soviet Union had just dissolved leaving huge areas of prime agricultural lands that had been confiscated from their original owners and made into large collective farms. All old fence rows, roads, and other benchmarks that allowed the small land parcels to be identified for each former owner had long since been removed. The government had made all the production and marketing decisions for decades. The former farmers had been transformed into farm workers. Some knew how to drive the outdated and poorly maintained soviet machinery, but they did not know how to make decisions.   Much of this land was located on the huge Danube River. The quality of the soil was reported to be as good as any found in Iowa, Illinois, or Indiana. It was relatively flat and rich and mostly unplanted since the fall of the Soviet Union. Land that had belonged to several hundreds of small farmers before the land was converted into a collective farm. It was now one large seamless field with no identifying markers other than its border fences. Individual farmers couldn't identify exactly where their land lies. Each aggregate farm could encompass a few thousand acres with each individual farmer owning a few acres.

To manage the interests of the individual farmers, the former collective farms had been converted into an organization like a cooperative. The land that, many decades ago, had comprised hundreds of farms would now be managed as one individual farm. At the end of the process, profit would be distributed according to what percentage of the total farmland each small farmer was estimated to have owned. The American entrepreneur would only deal with the leader of the cooperative, not the individual farmers. The cooperative deal with the individual farmers.

The government had installed a system of gigantic pumps along the Danube that pumped unimaginable volumes of water from the river into distribution tubes that took water to every acre of land for miles. It was an engineering marvel and had been unused since the fall of the Soviet Union.

There was no marketing system in place. There was no money available to pay for the needed resources. There were no chemicals or appropriate seed or equipment in-country that would be needed to put this unused land back into production.

There was no infrastructure to take all the corn that could be raised away from the fields and to any place that could consume the corn. Romania needed someone to hook these unused resources together and make them work. That was the purpose of this huge project.

The American entrepreneur then revealed the scope of the project. I can no longer remember the exact numbers, but I know it caught my attention. They were to be six farm managers. As a farm manager, I managed 60 farms, but I had not been responsible for the machinery, equipment, and other resources. If I assume that each farm manager in Romania would be responsible for ten farms that should be reasonable. If it could be reasonable that each cooperates could total four thousand acres, then we could expect the total acreage to be nearly one-quarter million acres for the project. This project, if assumed to be a square, would be 20 miles by 20 miles.

The resources required for such a large project were staggering. If center pivots were used, 150 units would be needed. Each four-thousand-acre cooperative was calculated to need two discs, one planter, three tractors, one sprayer, and one combine. Totaling this, the project would require 180 tractors, 60 planters, 60 sprayers, etc. All equipment was to be bought from John Deere and all seed and chemicals were to be purchased from Pioneer and Monsanto.

Planting was to start in April and May of 1999. All tractors, implements, and materials had already been shipped. The project manager was nervous that some unforeseen event would prevent the shipment from arriving on time in Romania.

Part of our job as managers would be to train the workers to assemble and test the equipment to ensure that it would work the first time when taken to the field. The schedule was a tight one.

All the other people also interviewing for these jobs knew the uncertainty of working in a foreign country. One problem would be that Romanian politicians could easily hold up the shipment once it arrived in port with the expectation that huge bribes would be paid to them to release the equipment and material due to the time sensitiveness of the process. When we voiced these concerns to the American entrepreneur, he calmed our worries by saying that he already owned a general who, if any delays occurred, would see to it that his material would immediately clear all customs requirements. This was entrepreneurial-speak for he had already paid for an overthrow of the government if it should become required. Should any politician place any barriers in the path, and the Romanian President did not remove them, a revolution was one short phone call away. The equipment and material would clear customs the very day they arrived at the Romanian port, or else.

The six American farm managers would be necessary for the life of the project: five years. After five years, the equipment, machinery, and tractors would revert to the ownership of the individual cooperatives. By that time, the cooperative members should be skilled in the use of the machines and in making managerial decisions. They should be able to manage the cooperative unit. The American entrepreneur would then only be responsible for the marketing of all grain produced by all the cooperatives. He would have a system of grain elevators installed and working that could take the grain to the Danube and then onto a seaport for sale on the world market. He would determine the price paid to the farmers for their corn. All corn had to be sold to him.

The above description should be reasonably close to what happened. My memory is hazy on many of the exact numbers, but my summary should provide a general idea of the scope and nature of the project.

As for us, the farm managers, we originally were to work eleven months a year with one month of paid leave to visit our families. Our positions were to exist for five years. Whether any one man chose to stay for the entire five years was his decision. Each manager would have a translator following him around. He was not expected to learn the Romanian language, which is a romance language. Many words look like those used in Portuguese—more so than Spanish. As for where we would stay, they were going to clean up a machine shop, replace the broken windows, find cots for us to sleep on, and settle all of us in that shop, dormitory-style. I imagined that to be a bit chilly during the winter months and hot during the summer months, but it would save the company money. The company could hire a cook to prepare food for all the managers. This arrangement did not suit me at all. I wanted to learn to speak the language. I wanted my small apartment with a part-time cook (lunch and dinner), but this was not going to be possible. I was disappointed.

After our orientation was over, we set out to visit some of the cooperatives that had already signed a contract with our American businessmen. We squashed into a couple of cars and started down a narrow highway bordered closely by trees that would have stopped any car or truck that left the highway unexpectedly. There were telephone poles along one side of the highway. On top of each pole was a huge nest occupied by a stork. Huge crows flew around the skies, cawing constantly.

We visited the Danube area. The land was flat. The water pumps were the largest in the world for irrigation, and to think that they had not been used since the Soviet Union disintegrated! We stopped near one field. The soil was very wet, too wet to be worked, but in the field was a tractor trying to plow. The tractor was slip-sliding around with its tires throwing mud in all directions. No American farmer would have been working the soil when it was that wet.   All the other candidates walked into the field to see the mud up close. I did not leave the highway. I did not want that thick and heavy mud on my shoes. I did not want to have to clean them afterwards. I stayed back. I could imagine what the mud looked like. Anything they said in the field could have been said on the highway.

We had been checked into a pension: a large house with many bedrooms for rent. It also had a dining area where all three meals could be taken. I had a roommate from Texas. He had spent five years in Saudi Arabia managing large alfalfa plantations with center pivots to produce alfalfa for dairies. He was a good man and very competent.

I spent several hours at a dining table where the project manager was interviewing representatives from cooperatives where they were hoping to obtain one of the few remaining slots in the project. Most of the candidates for farm manager were also present. For some reason everyone smoked. Not only did they smoke, but they chain-smoked. The room had smoke hanging from the ceiling. I changed positions several times, but no matter where I sat, smoke was being blown into my face. No matter how much I tried, I could not understand what was happening. It was a procedure that I could not nail down.

One day, I was told that that afternoon we would be going to visit a cooperative in the rural area. We would meet with the entire cooperative board of directors. When the time came, we all loaded into a couple of jeeps and we were off to this cooperative. After a time, we turned from the road and we were told that we had arrived. I was ready to climb down from the crowded jeep which was also filled with smoke. I was tired of breathing smoke and having smoke blown into my face.

When we climbed out of our jeeps, I looked around and saw what I thought was a junk yard with abandoned tractors, combines, plows, discs, and other equipment. It was, in fact, the equipment that the communal farm had used to farm the few thousand acres that the communal farm owned. Across the yard was a three-storied building that was at least three hundred feet long: the farm's housing for the members of the communal farm. In another direction was the business office for the commune.

We were directed towards the business office. I could not wait to get inside because it was bitter cold outside, and the breeze did not help. My fingers were already tingling from the cold. We entered the business office single file and were directed onward to a meeting room. The ladies working in the main office were anxious to get us through their workspace so they could close the door. The board members were already present and had selected their places at the long table.

The meeting room was from forty to fifty feet long and no more than eight feet wide. There was a narrow table stretching from end to end with chairs on both sides. In the middle of the room was a small coal stove, which was not lit, and would not be lit. We were informed that it was broken. It was nearly as cold inside as it was outside. Everyone's breath created fog. When people decided where to sit, no one removed their jackets or gloves. Finally, as people were making their opening statements, everyone lit a new cigarette. Everything that was said had to be translated since we did not understand Romanian and the Romanians did not understand English. I was miserable. All the smoke seemed to be drawn to my nostrils and mouth. I could see myself being diagnosed with lung cancer when I returned home. I could no longer see the people at the other end of the table due to the smoke hovering heavily in the air.

The meeting continued for what seemed like hours. I had trouble paying attention and dreamed about returning to the warmth of my pension room. I was losing my enthusiasm for this job. I had limited mechanical ability. I did not think I would be able to work with a team to assemble all that equipment. I did not want to live with my colleagues in a dormitory setting, especially when that dormitory was a converted machine shop, or storage shed, whatever it was because it was still unclear to me what it was. And now, I could barely see the person seated across the table from me. I wanted to go home.

Finally, the meeting ended. We all shook hands with each other, and we worked our way out of the meeting room through the business office where the women tried to hurry us along to leave so they could again shut the door. We loaded ourselves into the Jeep and returned to the pension. There was much talk, but I had difficulty understanding the nuances as to what had been accomplished and what had not been accomplished. In fact, I did not care. I had my doubts if I wanted to have this job or not. It did not seem so attractive as it once did.

During some spare time, I walked around the city. I found the entire region to be ugly and depressing. There were no bright colors other than black. The clothes were black. People wore black shirts, black coats, black shoes, black pants. Everything was black, even the snow was black due to coal dust in the air and pollution that settled on the snow and turned it black. If you rubbed your hand over a car's paint, your hand became black.

I checked with a Realtor to see how much an apartment would cost to rent. I asked to see the best: "apartment typo Americano." The real estate agent drove me to see an apartment in a building that had about fifteen floors and was longer than a football field. When she opened the door to the apartment, there was a hallway that was about five feet wide and ten feet long. Directly in front of that was a kitchen that was about five feet by eight feet. It included a kitchen table. People ate in the kitchen. Alongside the kitchen was a bathroom that was about five feet by seven feet. At each end of the hallway was a bedroom. Each bedroom was about nine feet wide and fifteen feet long. The entire apartment was about fifteen feet by twenty-four feet for a total of fewer than 400 square feet. This was a large apartment, and it had no living room. This was another disappointment.

Talking to the real estate agent, I asked several questions. She explained that one problem had been that three renters in the building were more than two months late paying their heating bill and the state-run utility company turned off the heat to all residents in the building; every single person in the building had their heat turned off because three residents failed to pay their bill. The real estate agent said that it was not really a problem because a few people always came forward and paid the debt owed so that, after a week or so, the utility was always restored.

I returned to the pension and learned that the project manager was going to choose his farm managers that evening. We also learned that the job was now considered a part-time job and would start in the spring preparing the equipment for the season and end in the fall with the caring for the equipment after all corn had been harvested. The farm managers were expected to return to the USA and be unemployed during the off-season. The salary range discussed was absurdly low. I was no longer interested in the job. I had a family to support and I could not do it with the wages they were offering.

The project manager continued that the two candidates that are not selected would return to the US the next day. Evening came and he called the candidates to his table-office one by one and talked with each person about ten to twenty minutes each. When he called me to the table, he told me that I would be leaving the next day. He had no more to say. I was not selected. I was not disappointed. In fact, I was relieved. I did not like Romania. I was afraid that I did not have the mechanical skills needed to put all the equipment and implements together. I did not like living in a dormitory-style machine shed and the salary was not commensurate with what I needed. But still, I had won something because I had now been to Romania and collected some adventure memories. I was happy. By this time, I just wanted to be home.

The next day, I was handed my airplane ticket home. I flew from Romania to Frankfurt, Germany where I spent the day and night. I arrived in Frankfurt an hour after my flight flew from Frankfurt to Chicago; therefore, I had to wait all day and spend the night in a motel outside of the airport in Frankfurt.

I was miserable there. I did not understand German. I had TV, but they had few English channels, and they were soap operas. The only channel worth watching was BBC and that channel recycled the news about every hour or two. I was bored and slept as much as possible, and then I looked out the window at the flat grassland with houses and small businesses scattered about the countryside.

Finally, night came, and I slept and woke up to catch my flight home. I could not wait to see my wife and children. I was rested.

My Volunteer Trip to Moldova, December 2010

It was late October when I received my invitation for a December volunteer opportunity in

Moldova. I had to look on a map to see where it was located. Moldova was scrunched between Romania and Ukraine. After a little research online, I learned that the language was Romanian because they used to be part of Romania. Until the early 1800s, it was a principality of Romania. In 1812, the Ottoman Empire gave it to the Russians, where it remained until after WW I when it was returned to Romania. I think it was Khrushchev who carved it out of Romania during WW II for political reasons.

I was excited. My assignment was to estimate the cost of production for about ten or twelve vegetables grown in the field and in greenhouses in two distinct regions of the agricultural north of Moldova. I would be living with local families where I would have a translator to help and my own room. I also had to present my results on the last day to a group of local farmers, Extension agents, bankers, and other local leaders.

I was challenged and had to accept the offer immediately. I would leave the day after my last final exam and return on Sunday before my first lecture in January during the new semester. I would have to have all my final exams graded quickly, calculate and post the final grades while packing for my trip.

I flew from St. Louis to New York to Vienna to the capital of Moldova. I arrived around 9:00 p.m. By the time I collected my luggage, passed through customs, and arrived at my little room in a small hotel, it was nearly 11:00 p.m. I was starving and excited. The translator wanted to go home. She had already put in a 12-hour day and was tired, but I was wound tighter than a drum. I asked if I could eat something and have a drink to slow down.

We crossed the street to a small bar and grill. I ordered a vodka and asked to see a menu. She preferred not to drink—she just wanted me to go to bed so she could go home. After two vodkas, she suggested that I order something to eat because the grill was shutting down. I was too excited. Recognizing her need to sleep, I allowed her to go home while I stayed and drank more vodka to relax. Eventually, the bar closed, I paid my bill by looking at the number on the ticket they gave me. I crossed the street to my hotel. My body was beginning to crash. I had been up for more than 24 hours. And now, I was hungry.

The next morning, I arose early, showered, and ate the breakfast offered by the hotel. It was delicious with all sorts of pork, cheese, toast, and excellent coffee. The translator arrived with a car and driver and we departed the city north to my first work location, which was almost on the border with Romania. I settled into a small room in a family's small apartment. The poor translator was cramped into an even smaller room.

The driver returned to the capital. The translator called our host organization and a car appeared to drive us to the first farmer's property. He had many acres dedicated to vegetables plus fourteen primitive green houses. The farmer invited me into a little trailer parked near one greenhouse. It was about eight by ten feet. Once inside, he directed me to sit in a chair pushed back from a small table. On the table were several trays. Some trays contained no fewer than five or six types of pork, scrambled eggs, and a host of other items that I did not recognize and coffee. It was very cold inside the trailer, but I felt that the heaters were on. I ate another breakfast so as not to embarrass myself. The owner was proud. All the pork cuts and other items had been produced on his farm.

After I ate, he asked me if I would like to see his production facilities. While a worker cleared the table of food, we exited the trailer and went to one extreme side of his old sheds.

There he had a few milk cows and calves. Next to them were a half dozen sows and little pigs.

There were a couple horses and many chickens running around.

He asked me to follow him to another shed. He had a garden tractor there, but not like our John Deere tractor. This one was one you walked behind and held two handles. It was much less expensively constructed than the garden tractors used in the US. He used it to plow and, to some degree, cultivate the greenhouses. He also used it to pull a small wagon around to collect the weeds pulled from each greenhouse.

In his yard were two much larger tractors. One, much older, probably had about sixtyfive horsepower. The other, a new Belarus tractor with about one hundred horsepower. This brand was the equivalent of a John Deere in the old Soviet Union. It was the best available.

He then took me down a path that had greenhouses evenly spaced on each side. They were about twenty feet by 120 to 150 feet each. The structures were constructed from wood and plastic. The plastic mostly had to be replaced each year. The soil acted as the floor. They were inexpensively constructed but likely generated a handsome profit. That was part of my assignment—find out how much profit they did generate.

One greenhouse acted as a greenhouse to the other greenhouses. It had a furnace that burned dried weeds, lumber, and any tree trunks available. This greenhouse had one end located much lower than the other end. The furnace was located at the lower end. When it was activated, the heated air rose and crept to the high end of the greenhouse. This allowed the farmer to start his seedlings as early as mid to late February. In Moldova, it was still very cold. By the time the weather had warmed enough to make the furnace unnecessary, he had seedlings well on their way in physical development. This allowed him to gain two weeks to a month on the other greenhouse producers in marketing the vegetables. Prices during this short phase were much higher than during the rest of the season when every producer was taking vegetables to market.

This producer was smart.

After we completed my tour of the facilities, we returned to the tiny trailer. It was warm, so he turned off the heater and turned on the lights. I explained to the farmer what my host organization had told me what my assignment was. I asked him if he also understood my assignment to be that. He clarified what he wanted. I explained to him that I had to ask thousands of questions to be able to fulfill my assignment. I asked for his patience and understanding and started my questioning. I asked in English. My translator repeated everything in Romanian. We waited while the farmer thought and then he answered. My translator converted it to English. I wrote it down and either asked a follow-up question or asked another question. It was tedious. It did not take long for me to have a headache. I started taking my headache pills.

After a couple hours, we were all cold and tense. It was time to take a break. A worker appeared with cookies, biscuits, and coffee. We turned off the lights and turned the furnace on. It was wonderful. I usually opted to step outside and stretch my legs.

At noon, the trays of pork, chicken, and a host of other plates were spread on the small table. I ate my fill while the trailer warmed up from the furnace. And then we started all over again.

This continued past dark and on to six p.m. when the driver came and took us back to our temporary apartment. The apartment owner was preparing dinner. It smelled delicious. I was ready to eat, but first, she served each of us with a 12-ounce glass of red wine. It tasted delicious. The translator carried on a conversation with the apartment owner as she prepared our meal before stopping to translate bits of her conversation. She explained that the apartment owner had made the wine herself. She wanted to know if I liked it. Also, the translator explained that homemade wine did not have all the preservatives that store-bought wine had; hence, it did not result in hangovers.

After dinner, I set up my laptop computer and opened Excel. I had to find some way of modeling each of the two systems of producing vegetables: greenhouse and field. That first night I was overwhelmed as I started to set up the depreciation of the buildings, greenhouses, machinery, and implements. I had to set up the cost centers and the income centers and the profit centers. I had to have a system for purchasing inputs and then adding the transportation cost and labor for handling the individual items and then calculate the cost (material plus transportation plus handling).

Working with the cost of field production was not so bad. I had done that before. The important step there was to have carefully delineated each field operation for production, such as field cultivation, disking, apply chemicals, planting, cultivation, and transporting the harvest. Then came the marketing operations (or post-production operations), such as transportation from field to farm, transportation from farm to market, and storage.

I worked late into the night on setting it up on the computer. I was worried because time passed fast, and I had to present my conclusions soon.

I slept like a baby. The next morning, we ate breakfast quickly at the apartment and were off to the tiny trailer again. I had a list of questions to clarify from yesterday's interview. Then, on to new questions. And so, it went for several days, each night I worked on the Excel models used to estimate the cost of production and then apply different sets of conditions to that model so that I could estimate the cost of production under varying conditions. Each day the model improved; even though I would hit a snag that might take a couple of days to resolve, or in a worst-case scenario, I would have to work around that unsolvable problem and find another way to do it.

One day, before lunch, the translator told me that we had been invited to a family lunch where all the farm workers would have lunch together. The reason was that the farmer's mother had passed away one year earlier, and it was the first anniversary. Everyone was walking toward a building. We followed.

When we entered the building, we were inside a narrow and long room with a long table filled with food and plates. We were seated at the end of the table opposite the farmer. Each plate had two-twelve-ounce glasses. One was filled with water and the other was filled with red wine. We stood behind our chairs while everyone prayed, then we sat. The men and women started on their wine while they waited for the plates of food to be passed. There was no space left on the table large enough to sit a saltshaker.

Once the food had been passed, the conversation started. I lost track of how many times the wine glasses were filled and refilled. Somehow, the stories focused on the times they lived under Stalin's reign. They talked of aunts and uncles and cousins who walked among them one day and then Stalin's men came and collected them for some crime that they supposedly committed—and they either never returned, or they returned and were never the same again.

Many of them were taken to prison camps in Siberia where life was difficult beyond imagination.

I was impressed by everyone's attitude. They were not shocked or bitter. They were just relating stories as they remembered some of the people who were not at this celebratory meal. It was as if they were talking about a relative who went to collect the mail, but never returned, or returned with severe psychological problems. As more wine was poured, more stories were told. I remembered that the translator had told me that in Romania, Moldova, and Ukraine when parties were planned, the planners used a rule of thumb that 1.8 quarts of wine were needed per adult invited. From what I saw at this party, the rule was not far from the truth.

After about eight days, I had completed my work with the first farmer. I had found a way to estimate the price and production risk of producing by each method (greenhouse and field) and for each crop.

I moved out of the apartment and traveled to a neighboring village and moved into a house with a family. I would stay with this family while interviewing the second farmer. This family had two daughters: twelve and sixteen years old. Since the village had no school beyond sixth grade, they attended schools that went through high school in a small city. The house owner owned an apartment in the village with the schools. The two daughters lived there. The older daughter kept house, cooked, and took care of herself and her younger sister.

The man's wife was very distant and showed no desire for friendship or to even talk. She stayed in her corner of the kitchen and prepared food, washed clothes (by machine), and kept house. We had our meals at a long and wide table, which were always delicious with most ingredients homemade or homegrown.

The man of the house was a soft-spoken man with a master's degree in something. He earned about three hundred dollars a month. With this, he managed to buy a small apartment for his daughters to go to high school in a regional capital and buy a building in his village that he converted into a convenience store. He was making good money by hosting me and the translator. He was an entrepreneur on his way up the social scale.

The lot on which his house was positioned was about one hundred by one hundred feet. It had a small corn crib which was mostly filled with ears of corn. It had an outdoor one-hole privy. It also had another shed that was used as a storage shed and a pig shelter. He always had a sow producing piglets and raising them into full-grown hogs before they were butchered for family use. The family ate mostly pork and rarely any beef. They ate what they produced. In addition, there were a couple of rows of grapes tied up. Apparently, he too, produced a little wine each year. All the ground had been plowed the previous fall. Ashes from the house's wood-furnace were scattered in one part of the plowed area.

The house was about thirty by fifty feet. The combined kitchen and dining area were the largest room in the house. There was a bedroom off each side of the kitchen as well as an entryway into a portico, which contained the clothes washer and drier, a bathroom with a shower, and an exit from the house into the courtyard. This was the regular exit that the family used to go to the bathroom.

On the far side of the room was another portico that led to the front door. Another bedroom and living room exited the short hallway that led from the dining room to the front door. The computer, with its exceeding slow internet hookup, was in the girl's bedroom. The living room had a pull-out bed from a sofa, which was extended for my use.

The house's heating system was different from anything that I had before seen. It was heated by two small wood furnaces built into the wall. The kitchen was heated by a small stove that burned wood. The master bedroom and the girls' bedroom shared a furnace (a common wall) while the living room (my bedroom) and the translator's bedroom shared the second furnace. Each furnace was about twelve inches wide, fifteen inches high, and eighteen inches deep. They accommodated sticks that were no more than two inches in diameter and fifteen inches long.

They were very tiny logs. The most interesting part of the furnaces was their location. They were located within the wall separating the two rooms. Each wall contained a network of pipes that carried the heat throughout the wall. The wall was hot, and the heat radiated out. My bed was positioned so that my head was near the wall and my feet were far away from the wall. My head was often almost sweaty while my feet were cold. One mistake you did not want to make was to reach out and touch the tiles that had been placed on the walls.

One day the translator was cold. She lifted her blouse and sweater a bit and backed against her bedroom wall. The spot she touched was near the furnace. She yelled and sported a reddened back showing the outline of tile for a couple of days.

Two days before Christmas, the house owner disappeared into the backyard. I heard the grown pig squeal, as it had everyday when he fed him, but today the squeal was shriller and shorter, followed by silence. I was working at the kitchen table processing data on my laptop. An hour later the homeowner appeared with large plastic bags filled with different cuts of meat. He retrieved a small meat grinder and tightened screws to secure it to the table. He laid out a cutting board and cut the larger cuts of meat into smaller ones and, one by one, passed them through the grinder. That night for supper, we had sausage—fresh sausage.

On the first day at the new homeowner's place, the translator and I were taken to meet the new farmer, Dimitri, at his mother's house. Dimitri had a normal height and weight, was slightly bald, except for around the edges, and was powerfully built. He had dark eyes that twinkled when he spoke.

He immediately started to kid me, and I kidded him back. This was not normally done, but with him, it felt natural. I felt I already knew him.

We met at his mother's house, which was a tiny, tiny house. It had a living room/bedroom that was about ten feet by fifteen feet and a kitchen that was about eight feet by eight feet. The kitchen had a wood-burning stove with two places for kettles and pans. It had a small sink with a place to dry dishes once they were washed and a place to sleep that was no more than three feet by six feet. It would be my favorite place to sleep because it was the warmest. During the winter in Moldova, there was no characteristic more highly valued than warmth. There was a wraparound sofa in the living room that could sleep an adult and a child. It was farther from the wood stove, so it was not as warm.

The second farmer's mother did not break the five-foot height and was not overweight.

Her face was full of deep wrinkles and surrounded by the typical scarf that the grandmothers wore. She wore black stockings that disappeared under her dress leaving no spot exposed to the bitter cold of the Moldovan winter. When she smiled, which was often, only a couple of teeth were visible. Her clothes were either bright red or black.

Dimitri invited us to sit down at a table that was in the living room. His mother went to a cabinet located in the back of the room and retrieved a nice coffee pot and dishes. She made coffee and offered it to each of us. I felt like I was a king. I could not have been better treated. As we drank the coffee, I was anxious to hear what Dimitri expected us to accomplish during my stay, but he was not in a hurry to enter that discussion. Instead, he talked about his mother, who was still standing in the room, drinking her coffee from a far corner.

He was divorced. His former wife lived in Moldova in a regional capital city and worked in a regional capital city in Romania.

Dimitri's father had been a part of the Soviet Union's military. He died unexpectedly from an unknown heart condition in the early 1960s. Dimitri was only a young boy at the time. Dimitri told the story of how his mother had worked day and night to put food on their table during those difficult years, some of which dealt with food shortages. His mother listened intently, smiled, and shook her head as she relived the experiences as he told them. More coffee was poured.

When Dimitri felt comfortable, he discussed the details of what he wanted me to accomplish. He had built several greenhouses in which he planted tomatoes and peppers. He also raised barley, cabbage, rye, red beets, and sugar beets in fields totaling several thousand acres of land. He rented this land from small landowners. They did not know what to do with it because of the many years that had passed without their needing to make any decisions. They had been told what to do by the central government of the Soviet Union. Also, during the decades since the small farmers' land had been confiscated by the Soviet Union, all the landmarks that had allowed each farmer to identify his own piece of land had disappeared. Even though they owned land, they did not know exactly where it was.

Under the new Moldovan government, the old communal farms were treated like cooperatives where each member-owned so many shares of the cooperative based on what the records showed they used to own inland before the Soviet Union confiscated it. Entrepreneurs, like Dimitri, rented the land from the cooperative, and the cooperative then distributed the rent to each member of the cooperative. To make wise decisions, he needed to know the cost of production for each crop and the cost of his machines.

The next day, Dimitri showed us the equipment that he had bought from a few of the area communal farms when the Soviet Union broke up, which had been almost twenty years prior to my visit. He bought the equipment for next to nothing because no one knew the real value of the tractors and implements. He jumped in and made low offers, which were accepted. He had gone as far as he could with this old equipment. He would soon need to start replacing the already worn-out equipment. He was spending all his time in the winter repairing equipment.   An old wooden building no larger than twenty by forty feet passed for a shop. I saw an old combine's engine lying outside the shed on the ground as it waited for another overall before it could be used again. One question Dimitri had was, Was it even profitable to farm? Could he even afford to buy better tractors and implements?

We sat down in a building in which he was living with his twelve-year-old son and I started asked questions about fuel efficiency for each of his bulldozers which he used to plant and disc. For heavy work, he had a 350 horsepower four-wheel-drive monster tractor. I had taken an inventory of all his special equipment, like a sugar beet planter and a red beet planter. I started to calculate how much it cost Dimitri in equipment, material, labor, and other costs to produce each crop. I then started on the harvesting and marketing costs.

I learned that he often had labor problems. Once, when cabbage harvest time arrived, which is a was very labor-intensive and time-sensitive operation, Dimitri could not find any men or women interested in performing the tasks, even at double the wages. The men were more interested in drinking than working. The women followed the men. Dimitri had times when he disked much of his unharvest cabbage crop into the ground. How could I factor labor unreliability into the cost of producing cabbage?

I learned of another problem. To obtain a better price, Dimitri had signed a sales agreement with an organization in Belarus, a country that lies to the north of Moldova and Ukraine. When the cabbage harvest started, Dimitri started sending truckloads of cabbage north to honor his sales agreements. The Belarusian Company refused to accept the cabbage. Dimitri had to turn the trucks around to return to the Moldovan local markets and sell them as best he could because they had suffered damage due to the many hours and days on a bouncing truck.

How could I include marketing risk in any cost of production, even with signed marketing contracts?

Finally, I developed computer simulation models using Excel that would allow estimates to be made. They included depreciation costs using used equipment, but not ancient equipment like he was using. I included methods to include some elements of price and production risk; although, I had no way to include the risk that the labor market would dry up. Eventually, he may need to nurture labor sources external to Moldova.

A problem that all farmers had with selling in local markets was the markets' sensitivity to production, especially with the crop was perishable like tomatoes, peppers, and to some degree, cabbage. When the Belarus organization refused to honor the contracts that it signed, there was even more production destined to the small local markets, which dropped the prices even more than usual. To minimize his losses, Dimitri rented an old pork production farm. He cleaned out the housing units and stored his excess cabbage there. His plan was to slowly sell his cabbage to local markets during the late fall and winter; thereby, preventing the price from dropping as much during harvest season and taking advantage of higher off-season prices. Dimitri was a thinker. He was a true entrepreneur. If anybody could thrive in this environment, Dimitri could.

At night, Dimitri always came to visit the house where I was staying. He and the house owner were excellent friends. Every night they were pushing the twelve-ounce glasses of wine at me and watching me drink every glass. I had to smack my lips and declare each glass the best I had ever tasted to avoid insulting the host. Red wine had always given me severe headaches, but this red wine did not. I was told this was because it was homemade wine and did not contain preservatives.

After several days of drinking multiple twelve-ounce glasses of wine, I resolved to take a one-night respite from drinking. I needed to flush my system with water to avoid a multiday headache, which I could feel coming on. Dimitri was sitting opposite of me at the table and was unusually insistent that I drink the wine. I was equally insistent that I did not want any wine.

Finally, the house owner poked me and whispered to me that this wine had been produced by

Dimitry and he wanted me to taste it. I had no choice. Dimitri poured me a full glass of red wine.

He displayed a huge smile while he poured. I had to drink it down like I had been given a glass of water after working all day in the sun. I looked up and Dimitri had the fullest and brightest smile I had ever seen on another human. His eyes never blinked as he watched me empty the glass of his wine. Several more glasses followed. That night I had a wing-dinger of a headache, but I had a friend for life. Not a bad trade-off.

Every day I worked on my Excel computer models. The translator was working on translating the slides and graphs that already had been finalized by the previous farmer. Finally, the day came for my final presentation and all slides had been translated. We drove to the regional capital and entered a government building with a large meeting room. People were milling about and talking. I had no idea who most of them were. I laid my laptop on the center table as did the translator. We found the electrical outlets, hooked them up, and turned them on. As we waited for the computers to come online, we were introduced to the guests. Some were other leading farmers in the area, others were the city's top businessmen, and others I was not introduced to.

The presentation started. I made a generalized statement about depreciation. Not being accustomed to working in a free market, and most of the farmers were still working with old Soviet Union machinery, they had no idea what the real cost of machinery was; therefore, they needed to be aware of the concept of depreciation. I tried to explain what depreciation was and how it worked. I explained that we could not use actual data for depreciation because their equipment was already fully depreciated. Any further use of it was "by the grace of God!" Slide by slide, I made my presentation. The people seemed satisfied. A few asked for copies of my thumb drive. We were happy to accommodate them. They had just been overwhelmed with economic information. Without a copy of the thumb drive, the information would slowly leave their minds. I also left them with a publication by the University of Nebraska that showed the cost of production in Nebraska using different methods. It should be useful to illustrate how costs of production are calculated using different production systems. I felt that I more than accomplished my host agency's goals.

On my last night in Moldova, Dimitri organized a party for me at a local restaurant. He invited his former wife, the family that hosted me, and a few other people. We occupied the entire second floor of the restaurant. Much before any food arrived, the wine arrived. It was served in twelve-ounce glasses. I noticed that Dimitri's former wife was as beautiful as any princess. She had the darkest straight black hair that hung down her back to her buttocks. She also had dark black eyes. She wore much jewelry around her wrists and neck and sat by Dimitri and across from their ten-year-old son. Most people had already emptied their glasses a couple of times. Her son had a small glass of wine, maybe eight ounces. She pointed to the glass and ordered him to empty the wine glass. He said he did not want to drink. His mother insisted. His answer was, "but Mom, I'm only ten years old!" She responded with a firm, "drink!" He drank.

The music started and people got up to dance. Most of the children danced in a circle. The adults who had a partner danced with their partner. The single adults danced with the children in a circle. Eventually, I had no choice but to join the dancing circle. Dimitri and his former wife danced beautifully together. They were both excellent dancers.

Later, the food came. It was needed to balance so much wine consumed. It was a great party. One that I will not forget. Dimitry and I felt an affinity for each other. We were more than brothers. We were soul mates. I know he is doing fine. I wish him and his family happiness.

They have had a difficult life.

The next day I left the capital of Moldova and flew to Germany to the largest airport I had ever seen. I walked miles inside seeking my next flight to the USA. I could not find signs to guide me. It was like walking across a city while contained in a rat maze. At last, I found the area that I had been seeking, but I was dying of thirst. These airports had no water fountains. We had to buy water in food service places. I found bottles of water, but only small bottles—about eight ounces. They cost eight dollars. I knocked three off before my thirst diminished; although I was still thirsty, I had exhausted my Euro supply.

I found my gate, entered the plane, and before it took off, I asked the flight attendant for bottles of water. The rest of the flight was a piece of cake.

Living in Ukraine – A few Stories

My time spent in Ukraine was complicated. It can be divided into two categories: first, a volunteer trip where I worked on a dairy project in northwest Ukraine; and second, I made several short trips (ten to fifteen days each) to meet single Ukrainian women with whom I had been corresponding. Each trip was unique and gave me new insights into the country and its culture.

Working with Dairy Farmers in Ukraine

I hurried to finish the grading of final exams at the University of Southern Illinois Edwardsville. When that was done, I had to calculate the final grades, and then turn them in. Once that was accomplished, I rushed home to pack my bags. To be careful that I did not forget anything, I checked everything twice. I needed my laptop computer with the cord, my camera with a charged battery, and a battery charger. I needed my passport, proof of international vaccinations, billfold, cash, information on my project's details, and very importantly, a list of all

contacts with their phone numbers just in case my translator
did not appear on cue at the airport.

My path from St. Louis to Ukraine was the usual. I traveled from
St. Louis to Chicago where I caught a night flight to Warsaw,
Poland. From there, I flew to Kiev, Ukraine where I was to be
met by my translator. I waited anxiously by the baggage claim to
find my suitcases. I grabbed them, passed through customs, and
started looking for someone who might be a translator. So far,
all translators had been female college students who spoke four
or five languages fluently and another one or two good enough
for basic conversation.

As I exited the customs area, I saw a sign with my name on it. It
was held by a male, and by the looks of it, his age was well
beyond that of a college student. I waved at him and he
followed me until I was clear of the inner workings of the
airport.

After the greetings, he said he would take me to the office
where I would meet the people who created this project. It was
late morning. There, they informed me that we would take the
night train to Lutsk, which was located west of Kiev. Another
fifty miles west and we would be in Poland. Another fifty miles
north and we would be in Belarus; this was the extreme
northwest corner of Ukraine. Even though I had been up for
umpteen hours, I would have no rest during the day. We
finished the business with the project directors, and we were
free to eat lunch and spend the rest of the day as we saw fit,
until the train left at 8:00 p.m.

The translator took me to an outside flea market that was
spread across several blocks, including across train tracks,
sidewalks, and any other place that got in their way. It did not
seem to be well-organized or organized at all for that matter. I

loved the displays that showed material from World War II. There were helmets, knives, water bottles, and many other things from the Polish army, the German army, and the Ukrainian army. The Allies-Axis front moved across Ukraine at least three times during World War II.

The array of strange items available amused me. We stopped to view the wares of an unshaven middle-aged man. He watched me very closely as he sat in a squat position close to the tarp on which he demonstrated his wares. He did not smile as he puffed on his homemade cigarette. There was no kindness in his eyes. Suddenly, he stood up and wobbled. He held out the hand that held the cigarette and said something to me. My translator snapped to attention and said something to me that I did not catch. My translator rushed in my direction. As he did, so did the man who was demonstrating his wares. My translator told me that the man did not like Americans and that I should keep walking away. He would talk to the man. He told me not to go too far but go far enough that the man could not see me.

As I turned and started to leave, the man kept advancing toward me, still with his arm outstretched and his fingers trying to point without dropping the cigarette. My translator stepped in to keep himself between the man and me. The man tried to step around the translator, but my translator successfully blocked the man. I quickened my step.

After walking what I considered to be a safe distance, I slowed down and started viewing the wares offered in the market. I had never seen such an odd array of goods together before. One person might be offering pistols, kitchen silverware, a car battery, World War II helmets from various countries, military knives, paintings, and plumbing items.

Soon, I tired and walked into the street to find a nice position in the shade of a wide tree. I kept looking in the direction we had been, but my translator did not show up. I began to worry and started pacing while maintaining my position in the shade. After several minutes, I heard someone whistling. I looked around and seated under the same tree as I was pacing were two old ladies. They were displaying some wares. Each woman had a comfortable chair and between them was a small table with a cloth-covered tray on the top shelf.

I looked at them as I pointed at myself. One nodded yes and waved me to approach them. I looked in the direction from where I was expecting my translator and then cautiously approached them. They both smiled. One lady grabbed a small glass while the other reached into the middle shelf on the table and magically a bottle of vodka appeared. The glass was filled to the spilling point and offered to me. I noticed one woman wore excessive makeup. She had blue eyes, red cheeks, and lips with an abundant layer of skin-colored powder on her face. The other lady was plain.

I knew that there was no escaping drinking the glass of vodka. I did not wish to offend them. I accepted the glass and held it high and we clicked glasses and drank. It was strong and had a kick. One lady picked up the tray on the top shelf while the other removed the towel covering it. It contained pieces of sliced bread. They ate a piece of bread after they took each shot.

They spoke no English and I only knew a few words of Russian, but we all understood vodka. We tried to make conversation with our few words of each other's language, but it was not working. My experience had taught me that in such cases, relax, smile and laugh a lot. And, of course, keep accepting the full glasses of vodka. They were nice, friendly ladies.

The ladies were, shall I say, happy when I met them and now, I was happy, and they were ecstatic. I do not remember what we said to each other. After a few shots, I remembered to look down the street to see if my translator was coming. I would have been completely out of luck should I become separated from my translator, but alas, I saw him walking towards me.

When he arrived, I explained to him what had happened, and he translated to the ladies. They smiled as they looked first at the translator and then at me. One lady pulled out the almost empty bottle and offered him a drink. He cordially declined because we had to go to buy the train tickets.

We took a taxi to the train station to buy tickets. We learned that the good seats had already been purchased. This train was not a nonstop train. It stopped at every small town in its path. The ride was approximately twelve hours; although, it was less than three hundred miles. Perhaps because of the slowness of the train, the price of a ticket was low, allowing even the poor people to afford the tickets.

The rest of the car was divided into compartments that were about eight feet square. There were two beds at floor level and two beds on top. It was much more convenient to have a bed on the first floor because you could get into and out of them without effort and without disturbing anyone. To have a seat in the top bunk was less convenient because you had to step on the first-floor bed and throw yourself up. Even so, there was no handrail to allow you to pull yourself up. For an old, fat man, it was easy to jump down, although, I felt sorry for the floor planks that had to stop my descent. Getting into the top bunk for an old, fat man was almost impossible. Which beds were ours—the top bunks?

I was not happy that the translator had waited so long to buy the tickets. He should have known the demand for the floor seats was great. He apologized, but that did not help.

The train arrived and unloaded. We boarded our car. There was the equivalent of a flight attendant waiting to help us board, to find our compartment, and to answer any questions. She was well-dressed in a nice skirt, blouse, and hat. She was as well dressed as any airline flight attendant. As we entered the front end of the car, there was a pushcart with a large pot of hot water that could be used to make tea. There was an abundance of paper cups, sugar, and stir rods.

We could serve ourselves, or she would serve us.

We walked down the aisle until we found our compartment. Our compartment mates had already situated themselves in their bunks. They had stored their suitcases and were playing cards on the little table located near the window. There was little room left for our luggage. We struggled to find a place for it. That was when I had to turn my attention to occupying my bed. No one paid any attention to me as I studied my predicament. Finally, I took off my shoes and placed them on my bunk. I carefully placed one foot under the lower bunk bed's mattress and jumped. For a second, the only thing that was keeping me up was my supersized stomach that was hooked on my mattress's frame. Somehow, I managed to pull my feet up and land on the mattress. It gave me a sense of satisfaction for completing the task; yet, terrorized me when I thought how many times that I would have to repeat the task during the night due to my miniature bladder.

A short time later, the train pulled out. I felt better when I heard the clitter-clatter from the tracks. When I expected the train to reach a full gallop, it started to slow. It entered a village, stopped, and exchanged passengers and merchandise. Then, the whole process repeated itself: the slow exit from the village, a period of travel at a slow speed before it had to slow for another stop, and another, and another village. The process never ended.

At some point, I became tired of sitting on my bed. I needed to walk and empty my bladder. I had no choice but to leap from the top bed and put on my shoes. Putting on my shoes without a chair to sit down on was no picnic. I grabbed them and stepped into the aisle to find the best way to put my shoes on without anything to sit on.

I went to the back of the car to discover the bathroom. It was the same size as those in an airplane but consisted only of a small sink, handrails to hang on to, and a six-inch circular hole cut into the floor. The smell was strong and the planks around that hole seemed to be weakened from the years of people missing the hole. I hoped it would hold my weight. I cringed when I imagined myself falling through the floor of the train. I felt for the people that chose to walk on the rail line, as rural people often did. The smell must have been horrible.

I walked slowly to the other end of the car to fetch a small cup of tea. Anything to avoid returning to my upper bunk. While the sun was still up, I stared out the window at the passing countryside. It was an agricultural area. I remembered one week in sixth grade we studied Ukraine. There was a story as to how Ukraine was the breadbasket for the Soviet Union. A picture showed an old tractor pulling an old drill seeding some small grain. The tractor seemed at least twenty years old based on our level of technology at that time.

Eventually, the sun sets. I could not see much from the window, so I walked to the front end of the car to attempt to talk with the stewardess. Unfortunately, she did not speak English. Using hand signals, she showed me the hot water, tea, and cups. I returned to my compartment, removed my shoes, and tried to remount my bunkbed without putting my foot in the mouth of the person occupying the lower bunk.

After a couple of hours, the stewardess came through with our evening meal. It consisted of an apple, a cookie and a main dish. I was used to eating more, but it was more than adequate.

As soon as the sun rose, the same stewardess returned with breakfast. We had a small glass of orange juice, toast with tea or coffee. After we had eaten and the stewardess had removed all the remnants of breakfast, the translator informed me that we were about to pull into our destination.

When the train stopped, we grabbed our luggage and looked for a taxi. The translator gave the driver our address and we were off. We arrived at our destination, which was close to the downtown area, and we started to climb the stairs. Our apartment was on the third floor. I had to stop and rest a couple of times, but I made it. The main office had made this reservation for us. This was unusual because I looked around the apartment and found that it had three bedrooms, a large living room with a spacious kitchen. I had no complaints.

After a shower and a change of clothes, we were off to meet with our hosts, their equivalent to our Agricultural Extension Service and the local agricultural cooperative. We were escorted into a small conference room where we met the head of each service. We were informed that the transportation that we were supposed to have was no longer available. I had a small amount budgeted for taxis within the city. I was informed that I could use that to visit farms; however, I doubted that I could visit even one farm with that part of the budget.

They explained that after the communist party had claimed all the land to create large communal farms, they had eliminated border fences plus any trees that grew in the fence rows. What we had was large open farms with no way to identify the exact position of the small individual farms. The commune was worked as a single farm with all proceeds handed out to individual farmers by the cooperative.

Each farmer maintained one to four milk cows. Each farmer had access to a small area of pasture. They also used road ditches and any place where some grass grew to graze cattle. The problem was that these cows produced only a small amount of milk. The milk was usually sold at the local market which generated low prices. Since only a small amount of milk was generated by each farmer, they did not have cooling systems. The morning's milk usually was taken directly to the market while the previous evening's milk had been converted into cheese and delivered to the market with the milk the following morning.

My assignment was to find a more profitable way to market their milk. This was going to be difficult without any way to visit the farmers. We returned to our apartment and tried to figure out how we were going to approach this. To say the least, we were disappointed.

What we could do was to visit the local farmer's market. We took a taxi there and found it to be clean and well organized. The market was all inside a building, which was unusual. The countertops were all stainless steel and easy to keep clean. I started to take photographs. Once, I rounded a corner and came face-to-face with a hog's head hanging on a hook. I didn't see that coming.

I noticed that every time I took a photograph, the people turned their heads away. Since their heads were covered by scarves, they effectively prevented me from seeing their faces.

Another section of the market was for rabbits. They were already butchered with their pelts removed, all except for about a four-inch section on the rear left foot. I found that curious and asked the seller why that was. He said it was left on to prove that the meat was a rabbit and not a cat.

The most populated area of the market was the milk and cheese section. Usually, each seller had purchased the right to sell on three feet of counter space. The sellers were of two types. The first consisted of sellers who were also the producer. The second consisted of sellers who had purchased their product from farmers. They specialized in selling the product. They might have two or three units of counter space.

I continued to take photographs and the people all turned their heads so I could not see their faces. I asked the translator why this was. He asked a local person who responded that it was never good to have your photograph taken. Back in the day of the Soviet Union, having your photograph taken never produced a good result. Often people disappeared a few days after having their photograph taken. Since I was a stranger, they assumed the worst and made it difficult for me to photograph their faces.

We tried to find a seller who could and would answer our questions. As soon as I started to ask questions, a crowd appeared as people pushed closer to hear what I wanted. When I asked their selling price, their buying price, and how much they sold each day, they immediately assumed that I was from the government. They thought that I was developing a new tax that they would have to pay and clammed up. Thanks to a good translator, I received some useful information. He explained what I was going to do with the data and that the organization that I represented worked for the benefit of the farmer.

From the market, we traveled to the supermarket. It was the largest and most colorful supermarket I had ever seen. Near the cash registers, there were circular displays about five feet in diameter filled with candies of various types, all arranged for their colorful effect. My eyes were drawn to them and upon seeing the pleasing color arrangement, I smiled. Then there were the aisle stands filled with merchandise. They had an area to buy all manner of nuts. Another with all manner of cheeses, both professionally made and homemade. I was sure that they sold all the types of cheese that the small farmers produced. Then, I saw the yogurts. They had many types that were pasteurized and professionally packaged and other fresh cheeses that were not pasteurized and could be bought in bulk by using the available containers.

One corner of the market had the wonderful smell of fresh bread. They had at least a hundred different types of bread. I immediately grabbed a plastic bag and a plastic glove and started to fill it with the more enticing slices of bread. I could not wait to return to our apartment so I could eat them.

After visiting the supermarket, I had trouble finding a place to market the small farmers' milk and cheeses. The supermarket paid low prices for milk and cheeses. The market was already being supplied with every possible product in a safe and sanitary place, much of it was sold directly by farmers. I discussed this with my translator. We thought that maybe there could be room to sell these products to restaurants or small neighborhood markets.

We visited several restaurants and found that they already had their sources and paid low prices. I think the milk producers would have to find special customers who would pay extra for quality milk and cheeses and then strive to deliver what their customers wanted. It would take time and work, but it might be possible.

One mechanism for saving money would be in who delivered the products to the market.

Currently, many producers each took a few liters of milk and pounds of cheese to the market. They each used their time and paid for transportation. If they could combine their milk and cheeses at the farm, one person could pay for transportation and, thus, reduce their transportation cost to the market. Only this could represent significant savings.

Soon, we met another volunteer and his translator. He also had a small budget for visiting farms. If he and I combined our budgets and traveled together, we could visit a few farms located nearby. We visited the cooperative people and they made two phone calls. One was to a medium sized milk producer (about twenty cows) and the other was a cooperative with a few dozen members. We agreed to meet with them the next day.

We met in the center of town. The cooperative had contracted a taxi large enough to carry four passengers and we were off. The first farm had a few dozen acres, which was all pasture. It was good land, flat and fertile. It had a good stand of grass; although, there was some brush mixed in with the grass and the grass was uneven—some was being overgrazed while just feet away it was being under grazed. This usually resulted in a gradual degradation of the grass since the good grass was eaten into the ground and, was again eaten every time it tried to regrow and consequently grew weaker. The less desirable grass was left ungrazed and therefore grew stronger.

The farmer was middle-aged and was considered remarkably successful. He had built a beautiful new house made from locally harvested hardwood trees. It reminded me of a classic log cabin. The interior was a little rough, but all hewn from beautiful hardwood.

As we entered the house, we were invited to sit at the kitchen table, which was made from hardwood about two inches thick. We were introduced to his wife, who smiled and offered us tea. We accepted. We started talking about his operation. My suggestion was for him to cross fence his pastures into paddocks that were of a size that would take no more than two days for his cows to graze. The cows would be forced to eat the less desirable grass along with the juicy grass. The cows would not be in the paddock long enough for any grass to regrow and, thus, be eaten again. By so doing, the tasty grass's roots would not be required to supply the energy for the plant every couple of days to regrow its leaves, and in so doing, it would weaken and eventually, die. Therefore, the good grass could recover as quickly as the less desirable grass, and the pasture would not deteriorate.

The farmer listened to what we said, but in the end, I doubt that he was going to change his way of operating. People are like that: resistant to change.

We drove on to our next appointment. It turned out to be a small village. It had a church, a theater, a business center where the coop's business was conducted, and a small store to supply the area population with basic supplies. When we arrived, the women were all attending a church service. A couple of men came out of the administrative building. They introduced themselves to us and we greeted each other. They caught a woman on her way to the church and told her to tell all the ladies to quickly go to the theater for a meeting with strangers. We walked ahead to the theater. It had a nice stage with beautiful curtains and three or four hundred movie theater seats. We sat and waited for the women while the administrators started to explain the community's needs. We had no idea if anyone would appear.

After twenty minutes the women started to enter and take seats. They scattered themselves all around, never with more than two or three sitting together. Two stern-faced men entered and took seats along the wall in the middle of the theater. They looked out of place with all the other women filling the auditorium.

Soon, the women stopped coming and one administrator introduced us and gave the other American the microphone. He talked about the power of cooperatives and eliminating the middlemen because many farmers never took their milk and cheeses to town but sold it to a local middleman at a low price. Every time he mentioned eliminating the middleman, many women looked at the two men seated against the wall with serious expressions on their faces. By their expressions, I could imagine them going home and beating their wives, children and kicking every dog they saw. They did not impress me as being nice men. I learned later that these two men were the community's middlemen. They were not happy with us being there or with the direction that the meeting was taking.

When the head administrator handed me the microphone, I was not sure what to say because most of the producers did not have pastures. They grazed their one to four cows in road ditches or areas that were considered common grasslands. Being common areas, they were all overgrazed and of poor quality because everyone put their cows there for the free grass. The grass was always noticeably short and with little leaf area to produce new food, the plants relied on food stored in the grasses' roots. Soon, the good grass died and was replaced with stronger grasses of low quality. I know of no way to improve grass that is available for common grazing. Each cow owner tries to maximize his cows' consumption of free grass, and in doing so, the grass is grossly overgrazed and deteriorates into a patch of weeds.

One woman in the audience had made a couple of important statements that perfectly defined their problems. The other American suggested that she be the local leader and take responsibility for marketing the milk and cheeses for everyone in the community. She responded that that would be impossible. When asked why she said that no one would trust her. Another woman chimed in that she did not trust her as did still other women. The American coop man was taken aback at their open honesty about their mutual mistrust. I think this was caused by seventy years of communism because mutual distrust was necessary for survival.

In fact, a group of women offered both of us Americans an opportunity to manage their group's few thousand acres of land. They said they could provide the machinery and labor for a share of the crop, but we were to manage the land and market the crops. We both turned them down because when the first setback occurred in producing or marketing the crop, they would blame us and want to hang us on the town square. But the idea did fascinate me. That could have been a wonderful adventure.

I returned to my apartment very frustrated. It seemed that every solution to their problems created a new set of problems that were even more difficult to resolve. It was the first time that I felt that I could do nothing to help a group of people. If I could stay longer, perhaps three to six months, I might be able to help them. Their problems were not going to be resolved by a short visit.

The next day I met with the country's leader of their equivalent to the Agricultural Extension Service. She was a middle-aged lady who was also the head of Ukraine's communist party. She was heavy-set and jovial. She asked me questions about what I had learned so far and provided additional information on several aspects of the situation. I asked her for a time series for the prices of several products. She picked up the phone and ordered them. Within fifteen minutes I had all the data that I had requested. She made things happen. I liked her.

We took another train back to Kiev. We had top bunk seats and I arrived exhausted.

I tried to summarize my experience in a short document for the Kiev office. I was hard-pressed to create anything new. I felt that my results were weak, and I was embarrassed, but that was all I had. I made my presentation to the Kiev head office and caught my plane back to the U.S.A.

Visiting Women in Ukraine--The Economy

Many men of the world, especially from the United States, go to Ukraine to date women. This is because there are many more women in Ukraine than men. I am not sure as to why this is. After World War II, many men had been killed; therefore, there were more women than men, but that was a long time ago. There has been ample time to reestablish the normal ratio. Men may leave the country to work in the European Union and other places, but so do the women. Whatever the reason, there were many more women than men.

Another interesting fact is that Eastern European women like to date and marry men who are from ten to twenty years older than they are. Of course, some women like to date men that are only a few years older than they are.

Ukrainian women are very loyal to their men and love their husbands and children very much. There is nothing that is more important to them. Ukrainian women treat their men like royalty. Men make all the decisions.

Like most of the countries from the old Soviet Union, many men and women are alcoholics. Many cannot hold down a job or stand up straight enough to walk. Drinking in the streets and parks is legal. It is not unusual to come upon a dozen men sitting on park benches in one area with many empty bottles on the ground and one more in their hands. Once when I was passing through the park with Svitlana (mother) and Tanya (daughter), a group of men started to yell insults at me and started to follow us across the park. Svitlana just held my hand and told me not to look back and to walk fast. They caused no further problems.

Many families have no children. Most families have one child; however, a few have two children, and fewer still have three children. The population was in decline because of familial preferences for family size. They were worried because apartments were small, often with no more than 160 square feet per family member. Svitlana's apartment was considered large but is probably no larger than 800 square feet. It has three bedrooms but no living room.

It cost money to clothe and educate their children. It was difficult to earn more than three hundred dollars per month per person. Unemployment was high. People also worked more than forty hours per week. It was not uncommon for people to work fifty to seventy hours per week without the benefit of receiving time and a half. They may earn 300 dollars monthly, but they worked whenever their boss wanted them to work.

Schools are also not free. People must supply uniforms for each school and pay other fees that accumulate quickly. The cost of living is high relative to people's incomes. A pound of meat costs about the same as it did in the USA. Dairy products and eggs were also expensive. I have met women with their children who could not afford to eat any dairy products nor eggs. The meat was only available in their dreams. They lived on spaghetti with ketchup for sauce. Many people only had two or three changes of clothing. It was not uncommon for a person to wear the same clothes for a week, while their other clothes were being hand washed and then ironed with an iron heated on the stove.

Several years after my first visit, people had washing machines (no clothes driers) and electric irons. During the period immediately following the breakup of the old Soviet Union, the economies of all these countries were in shambles. The only way they survived was by three generations living in the same apartment. A few years ago, Svitlana lived with both her parents and her daughter in one apartment: hence, the three bedrooms.

Odessa—The City and Life in the City

Odessa is an old city—more than 2,000 years old. Its streets are narrow with many of them still covered in small stone blocks and are filled with potholes. Many streets are paved, but they also have potholes. There is some discipline to the traffic, but care must always be practiced because there are always those drivers who do not obey the rules. Most cars have a traffic camera to record what happens in front of the car. In case there is an accident the driver must show the police and insurance company what happened.

The older apartments are no more than two stories and are constructed from mud bricks. The walls are wide. I rented one apartment whose interior walls were four feet thick. They had high ceilings. I have seen ceilings that were at least fifteen feet high and could have been twenty feet high. This helps during the oppressive summer heat. A high ceiling allows the hot air to rise leaving the cooler air at body level.

The city had many statues of lions and historical personalities. Every city seemed to have a statue of Stalin, but there were others of generals and authors. Ukrainians love to read and give high esteem to their better authors. The city also had many small parks, each one with a statue of someone. It also had several larger parks filled with bushes and trees and flowers and cement paths for people to walk and benches to sit and rest. In the center, there was a place for a band or orchestra to play during the warmer summer months.

Odessa is a city that values the arts. They have a large and beautiful opera house. They also have a famous theater. These are not just for the rich and famous to watch, but schoolteachers, cleaning ladies, seamstresses, and other common people attend their performances. The cost of a ticket is low enough that almost everyone can afford to attend performances.

There are always musicians standing on the side of a high-volume traffic spot in a park or street. They have their instrument's carrying case open on the ground for people to place a coin or paper bill. Once I saw a young girl playing the flute. She was serious and always looked straight ahead. I prepared my camera and started to take photographs of her from all angles. She never broke her pose. She was very professional and played her instrument well. I dropped a nice bill in her flute case and left her alone with her thoughts and music.

The city also had its share of night clubs. These were places where the young single women frequented in their quest to find a suitable husband. They lined up against a wall and watched the people enter. They reminded me of birds perching on wires strung along with tall posts. I offered to take Svitlana and Tanya to a nice nightclub, but they preferred that I take them to the ballet.

Odessa is located on the north side of the Black Sea. It is located at longitude forty-six degrees north, which is approximately where St. Paul, Minnesota is located; yet, for the people of Eastern Europe, it is considered the Miami of the United States. During the month of August, without a reservation, there are no hotel rooms, apartment rooms, or space on any flight leaving Odessa. The city is filled to its brim with tourists; the streets are filled, and long lines exist for everything that tourists like to do. All bars and restaurants have extended their space to include the sidewalk and part of the street. They were all filled with happy patrons who were drinking, eating, laughing, and telling stories.

The city had many parks, but one was more visited than the others. It had a huge bronze chair on display. Its surface was rubbed smooth by the thousands of visitors who have sat on it for a photographic opportunity. In fact, a line had already formed by 8:00 A.M. One woman sat on the chair for a moment without anyone taking a photograph of her. She descended from the chair and stared at it for a long moment from one side, then she went to the other and stared some more before moving on. The chair represents a book from that title that is very well known in all the former Soviet Union's republics. All school children must read it.

Next to this chair was a long garden with flowers of many bright colors. Then, in the middle of the block, was a wooden bench with another bronze statue. It was of a man sitting on the bench with one leg placed on top of the other. Several places on the statue were worn smooth from people sitting next to the author or sitting on his lap. Often there were three people at once having their picture taken: one on his lap and two more on each side of him. The man had his arms stretched out and were laying on the top of the bench back. The two people on either side of him snuggled up to him like he was their father or grandfather. All the time there was much laughing in the lines of people waiting for their turn at the statue.

There was also a market along the many sidewalks that traverse the park. They sold cloth items, needlework, and paintings mostly that they made themselves.

On another side of the park was a curved bench raised a few feet off the ground. During the early evening, it filled with young people drinking beer (it was legal in Ukraine), telling stories, playing the guitar, singing, and laughing. Early one evening there were two young and beautiful ladies sitting by themselves and chatting. They were dressed in the gothic style, but they were clean, and their clothes were new as opposed to others dressed in Goth and they looked like they had slept in the streets. These girls were different.

I learned that they were students in the university in the field of economics. They spoke fair English and did not mind me asking questions about their lives.

Spread around the park were many statues of lions, generals, and famous politicians. People liked to approach them and touch their feet. They were usually on a pedestal located five feet from the ground. They even took photographs of these statues.

On another side of the street young adult males collected and drank beer. In front of the park benches lay many empty beer bottles. Their speech was slurred, and no one was smiling. To me, they looked unhappy and depressed. I learned to walk around them.

Dating Women in Ukraine

In the early days, I had corresponded with Svitlana and Tanya for months through short letters that were translated and delivered to Svitlana. We knew a little bit about each other when she agreed that I should visit her. This would be my first trip to Eastern Europe (other than Romania). I was extremely excited. I remembered in the sixth grade reading an article in our weekly news magazine that we received. It showed a photograph of an old tractor and drill in Ukraine. This would have been about 1959. I remember the land was flat like in my area of Nebraska.

I received my Visa for my passport, bought my ticket, and packed my bags. I flew from St. Louis to Chicago and then, on a much larger plane, on to Warsaw, Poland. That flight took ten hours. I changed into a much smaller plane to continue my flight to Odessa. The last flight segment only took one hour. I was so excited. I could not believe that I was about to become acquainted with Ukraine.

I was met at the airport by Svitlana and a translator. Svitlana was a beautiful blond. I was extremely impressed. I hoped that I had not been a disappointment to her. I was much older and fat.

The translator introduced herself and then she introduced Svitlana to me. I had to collect my bags and clear customs. Then we were off to a nice restaurant since it was already early afternoon. I had been traveling for fifteen hours and had spent twelve of those hours in the air. I had not slept on the plane and was exhausted. I was existing on pure adrenaline.

At the restaurant, both Svitlana and I did not know how to act or what to say. We were nervous. We started slowly and gradually to relax and laugh. I felt so strange.

After we ate, we decided to go for a walk on the beach. Even though it was May, with the strong breeze coming in from the

Black Sea, I was cold. I was uncomfortable and would like to have turned around and left. Svitlana did not seem to mind it much; although she did acknowledge that it was chilly. What was a short walk on the beach for Svitlana, was a long trek for me. I suffered from neuropathy on the bottoms of my feet; therefore, my feet always hurt, but after this long walk, it was painful. I suggested that we meet the next day.

I went home and messed around until midnight when I tried to shower. I discovered that there was no water and then the electricity disappeared. I learned that sometimes the city did that to save its water and the coal that is used to generate electricity. I adapted and took showers earlier and went to bed before midnight.

The next day Svitlana appeared with her daughter. I think she needed to meet me alone to determine if I was an appropriate gentleman for her daughter to meet. We went to an amusement park where Tanya could go on certain rides. The rides did not cost much, but they cost enough to make it impossible to do for a single mother.

After Tanya was tired of the rides, we decided to go to the beach and had lunch in a nice restaurant. Svitlana and Tanya sat next to each other and I sat on the other side of the table. Svitlana asked if she could order a bottle of wine. I agreed if she would select it. When the waiter came with the wine, Svitlana agreed that Tanya could have a small glass of wine. Svitlana was using this experience to teach her daughter how to be a proper young lady. She showed her what to do with the forks, the napkin, and how to drink wine. Tanya was fourteen years old, but in Ukraine, there was no law preventing a child from drinking alcohol.

On the next day, we agreed to take a day trip to Uman, a city located 200 miles to the north. It had a large park that was designed by a famous Polish architect in the eighteenth century when Poland ruled the region. The park was very green with many trees. It had a large lake with a fountain that sprayed water tens of feet into the air. It was not operated by any pump, but by gravity using water from another lake located at a higher location.

While walking around this large park, we discovered a boat ride down a narrow manmade channel. It was beautiful to see all the park's features. I was glad to be moving and sitting down. After a bit, we came to an underground tunnel. It was about the length of a football field and totally dark.

I was tired and anxious to go home, but Svitlana only sat and watched people. She and Tanya were having a wonderful time and did not want it to end. Finally, she gave her approval to head home. We started walking slowly to the taxi that had brought us.

During the trip home, no one spoke much. We were all tired. We arrived in Odessa at 10:00 P.M. I gave Svitlana money for a taxi back to her apartment. After we saw them enter the taxi, my taxi took me home.

The next day we had another day trip to the city of Bilhorod-Dnistrovskyy, which lay fifty miles south of Odessa, also on the Black Sea. At this site was a fort that was more than 2,000 years old. It encompassed four or five acres. Its walls were at least fifteen feet wide at the base and ten feet wide on top. They were also at least fifteen feet high. At the base of the walls was a channel that was filled with water from the Black Sea if the fort occupants were in danger of being attacked. This channel was at least ten feet deep and fifteen feet wide at the top. Any invader trying to breach the fort would have had a difficult time doing so.

On the inside, there was another wall separating one area from the other. This smaller area contained all the bunkers and castles and other stuff essential for the royals. The larger area was used for the common folk to bring their businesses and trades and grain stocks. The royals basically moved the city into that small area where they would live until the siege was over. Should the enemy break through the outer wall and conquer the local citizens, the royalty would close the big gate and defend the smaller inner area, which now contained all the military might and the royals.

It was satisfying to imagine everything that those walls had seen. Had the outer walls ever been breached? Had the inner walls ever been breached?

My Trip to Mariupol

On another trip, this time at the end of the fall semester in mid-December, I had as my destination the city of Mariupol. It was a small industrial city 350 miles east of Odessa and located on the edge of the Azov Sea. I remembered in high school looking at maps showing the Black Sea and Azov Sea. They fascinated me. I could not wait until I saw the Azov Sea. I had planned on taking a common bus on a twelve-hour bus trip to Mariupol. It would not leave until 7:00 P.M and it was barely noon. I did not want to wait seven hours for a bus and then take a twelve-hour bus trip. I was too anxious. I haggled with a taxi driver until I thought he was offering a reasonable price. The driver carefully loaded my luggage in his trunk, and we started down a narrow street. Some snowflakes were falling as we began our journey.

Once on the highway, our progress was good because the streets were, for the most part, clear. The driver sped along at a normal speed; although, he was cautious about occasional ice sheets. After an hour, the snow was falling at a quicker pace and the road began to have more snow and ice on it.

In Ukraine, I did not think they used snowplows, or they were used sparingly.

This road had not been plowed. The driver slowed his speed to match the conditions.   After three hours, our progress was compromised by heavy snow and thicker ice on the road. The driver's windshield wipers could hardly keep the windshield clean. The driver was worried; so was I. After the third hour, our progress was no more than twenty miles per hour. At that rate, we would not reach Mariupol until dawn. He started to float the idea of turning back. I could not accept that as a solution.

After four hours, it was turning dark and the driver was not concerned with my disagreeing with him. I understood that he was about to turn around, with me or without me. I did not want to be stuck in Ukraine at night in a snowstorm, so I offered him an alternative. We were a few miles from Melitopol, a small city. He agreed to take me that far. He even said he knew of a nice hotel and would take me there. I told him that he could keep the full amount of money that I had paid him to take me to Mariupol. He agreed.

The driver offered to help me check into the hotel and to call the lady I was trying to visit in Mariupol. I spoke with her, telling her I would be late. She offered to grab a cab and come to pick me up. All I had to do was wait for her to rescue me. I was only 150 miles from Mariupol. It would take her a few hours to reach me.

I checked in and took my luggage to my room. It was a cozy room. I tried to sleep, but I was too excited; even though, it had been much more than twenty-four hours since I had slept the last time. After a few minutes, I gave up, dressed, and went downstairs. I noticed that the hotel had a small bar. I entered and picked an empty table. Only two or three other tables were occupied by young people. I ordered vodka. I felt better. I ordered another vodka and I felt even better. That was when the big, strong Ukrainian woman who had checked me into the hotel came to my table. She told me that I should not drink alone. She said that she had to manage the hotel and could not drink with me, or she would. I bought her vodka and ordered another for myself. She stayed. In fact, she and I ordered a couple more vodkas, then she told me to go to my room because the bar had to close. She was nice about it, but she wanted me gone so she could do her work.

I walked slowly up the stairs to my room and prepared for bed. After an hour, I still could not sleep. I dressed and wandered downstairs again. The bar was closed, and all lights were off. Only a couple of night lights were on. The reception area was dark. I looked around. Behind a latticed wooden construction that went from the floor up to about ten feet height was a battery of four or five steam heaters used to heat the reception area. About two inches above the top of the steam heaters was a wooden bench with the boards each separated about an inch from its neighbor. I thought that looked like a nice place to rest. The heat rose from the radiators and passed around the boards and heated my body. I was in heaven.

Still, sleep did not come. I started singing little tunes and tapping my fingernails on the boards between me and the radiators. I must have slept some because I heard someone complain that if I did not be quiet, we both would be thrown out. I looked at the other end of the bench and a homeless man was trying to avoid the cold outside. I obliged him and became quiet. Then I began to wonder how I had understood him. I spoke no Russian and he, a homeless man, I assume, spoke no English. That mystery still bothers me today.

My friend, Marina, arrived at about 3:00 A.M. and we had no problem arriving in Mariupol with the taxi driver's safe driving. I went to my apartment where I crashed and slept for hours.

On December 21, the shortest day of the year, the sun rose at about 9:30 A.M. and by 3:00 P.M it was preparing to set. This surprised me.

Marina took me to a local market to buy supplies for my refrigerator. I took my camera to photograph the market. As we walked about buying things, I began to take photographs. The people would always turn their heads. People would always say something, especially the men. Marina would not translate what they were saying to me; however, she did ask me to stop taking photographs. The men began to follow us and talked loudly to me. They were visibly agitated. Marina grabbed me by the arm and rushed me from the market. She asked me to leave my camera at home next time.

One day Marina wanted to go for a long walk. Foolish me. I did not use a scarf or wear anything with a hood. All I had was a light coat, which was good enough for Illinois weather, and we were off. She grabbed my arm and we started walking on a narrow street that lied one hundred feet from the beach. We followed the street. There were no buildings that separated us from the blistering wind coming from the Azov Sea. I was shaking as I walked. She asked me if I was cold. Of course, as a man, I could not impress her by telling her that I was cold, but I was. We walked on and on and on. My feet were hurting, my face was frozen, and I was extremely uncomfortable. Finally, she suggested that we turn around. Before we turned back, she turned toward the beach. We walked toward the water. We were walking on the sand, just out of reach of the water. Nothing protected us from the open sea breeze. I was mind-numbingly cold. I was sure I was not going to complete the little "walk-about." I did survive, but I never left the apartment again without a scarf and headgear that would keep my head and neck warm. My coat and gloves offered inadequate protection against the cold, but there was nothing I could do about that.

On Christmas Eve, Marina, her son, and mother came to my apartment for a feast that had been prepared by Marina. As she made the last preparations for our meal, I brought out my vodka bottle. I was disappointed to discover that it was nearly empty. That was when I discovered that grandma had brought her own full gallon jug of homemade vodka. I think she made it from wheat. Seeing our predicament, she offered us some of her stash. Marina warned me to be careful. I should have taken her advice. We filled our shot glasses and as I raised my glass to my lips, I inhaled before emptying the shot glass. I thought I was going to die. As I inhaled, the fumes entered my lungs and burned them severely. I could not talk or breathe for a long moment. Marina saw my predicament and offered me a piece of bread to take the bite from the experience. It was then that I learned to exhale before raising my shot glass. Using this new drinking technique, I was able to take a few shots; however, it was meant only for the strong.

Grandma drank it like water.

Grandma, witnessing my initial failure at drinking her vodka, laughed at me and said she only drinks her homemade vodka. She refused to drink that weak store-bought stuff. It was good because the more grandma drank, the more talkative she became. Soon, she was talking about her displeasure with the breaking-up of the old Soviet Union. It made the trains run on time and it was inexpensive to travel by train or bus. You could visit all the countries in the Soviet Union without visas and without being stopped at the border. The medical treatment was better and there was less corruption in the government. The education system was better. She said there were no unemployed people and no homeless people. She went on and lamented that today, many young people disrespected Stalin. These kids should be severely punished until they show the proper respect for the greatest man in the Soviet Union. I only listened, but I found her comments interesting.

My Trip to Voronezh, Russia

I had made friends with a lady who lived in Voronezh, Russia. I decided to visit her for ten days one March a few years ago. This city was located three hundred miles south of Moscow. It had one million inhabitants and was five hundred years old. The city straddles the Voronezh River which drains into the Don River, which drains into the Black Sea.

I flew to New York and then to Moscow. I arrived in the morning. My next flight to Voronezh was from an airport across the city and at 8:00 P.M. I had most of the day to kill. I was met at the airport by a driver. His job was to show me Moscow during the day and then to take me to the other airport in time for me to catch my flight.

The driver took me to the train station. This was fascinating to me. It was huge. Russia counts on its trains to carry many passengers and freight since it is the cheapest form of transportation. I remember watching old war and spy movies. There were always trains involved. What I remembered most was the shrill sound of the trains' whistles. I always knew that something bad was going to happen when the train blew its whistle.

From the train station, we drove to the Kremlin. It was gigantic with a large parade ground between the church, the

Kremlin, the KGB, and another large government building. I walked around the parade ground. It was too cold to be comfortable; yet I saw limousines driving up, parking, and expelling large numbers of people from wedding parties. Everyone had trouble standing upright from being drunk; even the brides had difficulty staying upright. The bride had no coat on, only her wedding dress, and the groom only had his tuxedo. The groups were incredibly happy with laughing by everyone. As soon as one limousine pulled out, another would pull in.

About 4:00 P.M. we started to the other airport. Moscow's traffic was notoriously slow. We traveled on snow-covered cobblestone streets, often with large potholes. Still, we arrived in good time at the airport. I grabbed my bags and headed into the large airport. This airport served mostly domestic flights while the other airport served mostly international flights. I looked around and found the check-in booth, but it was closed. I assumed it would open around 6:30 P.M. I went to a place to sit and wait for the booth to open.

At 6:30 P.M. I returned to the check-in booth and found it still closed. I waited. After several minutes, I saw someone who worked for an airline. I stopped them and asked them when the booth was going to open. They told me that it had opened and had already closed. I panicked. The lady told me not to worry. She would take me directly to the boarding area, but she added that we would have to hurry. She took off walking at a fast pace. I tried to keep up as I pulled my suitcase and carry-on while my laptop and camera swung from my neck. The airport was full.

People were everywhere, including sitting and laying on the floor. Progress was not easy. First, we had to go through security. The line was exceptionally long. She motioned for me to follow her. She marched up to the front of the line and spoke into the ear of the person controlling the line. That person

opened the ribbon and motioned me into the front of the line. I
had to send my suitcases through the line, take off my belt,
shoes, remove my computer from the carry-on. Of course, my
suitcase triggered a beep from the machine. I had to grab my
belt, shoes, and computer plus my suitcases and pull them to a
side table where I was asked to open them. One person
diligently searched both cases and motioned me on. I just
managed to return my laptop computer and close both cases
when my guide waved for me to follow her. I had to hold my
paints up, hold my belt and suitcase and run after my guide. We
went around people, over people and the crowd noticed my
predicament and cheered me on.

After what seemed like forever, we arrived at the boarding gate.
It was about to close. The receptionist radioed to hold the bus
for one late passenger. She processed my ticket as I weaved my
belt on and put on and tied my shoes. I thanked everyone and
hurried down the hall and down the stairs to an outside door
with a bus parked in front. I jumped onto the bus and we
departed for our plane, which was somewhere down the
airstrip.

Finally, the bus pulled along the side of a small, two-
engine propeller plane that looked like it had been
manufactured before World War II. As we exited the bus, we
had to be incredibly careful because we were stepping on slick
ice. We had to take exceedingly small steps to minimize our
chance of falling. I felt lucky when I reached the stairs without
falling. I climbed the stairs and leaned over to enter the plane. I
saw two flight attendants helping people. There were only a few
seats, maybe twenty. We did not have assigned seats so finding
our seats was easy. The seats were old, dirty, and well worn. I
began to question the quality of the airplane's maintenance.

As we passengers seated ourselves, someone was
throwing the bags into a space located between the pilots'

cabin and the passenger space. When they finished loading, the passenger door was closed. It took two or three attempts to secure it. My thoughts returned to the quality of the airplane's maintenance. Then one flight attendant went to the front of the cabin and wired the door shut. I was now officially frightened.

I did not speak Russian and these flight attendants did not speak English, since it was a domestic flight. The flight attendants handed out pieces of candy then they gave, what I imagined was, the "in case of emergence" speech. What I interpreted them to be saying was, "in case of emergency, a crucifix will drop from the overhead position. You should kiss it and then bend over and kiss your ass goodbye because we most likely are going down..." At least, that was what I imagined.

We taxied to our runway and waited for our turn to take off. The pilot had been playing with one engine and then the other by racing them. My confidence was not enhanced. Finally, we raced (kind of) down the runway and were airborne. We did not fly at a high elevation. I could see streetlights and car lights as drivers raced down the highway. I do not know what our speed was, but it took one and a half hours to fly 300 miles.

My mind focused on the sound of the engines. Occasionally, one engine would miss a few beats and fall silent. The sound of one engine beating is fine if you are in a single-engine plane. It is not comforting when you are in a two-engine plane. Inevitably, the engine would catch its breath and return to its regular beating, but then the other engine would pause. I really was not comfortable with this flight. I sucked on the candy and continuously asked the flight attendants what time it was.

Finally, I felt the plane's altitude start to decrease. I looked out the window and saw a city's lights ahead. We were arriving! The plane continued to lose altitude and close the distance to the city. I felt the wheels touch the runway, but when the plane slide sideways, I realized it had only touched the ice on the runway. The plane recovered and taxied down the runway until it was across from the airport terminal.

It stopped and quickly opened the door. Since I was not the first to descend the steps, I saw a string of people walking from the plane to a bus which was parked about 150 feet away. Why it was parked so far away, I did not understand. When I took my first step on the ground was when I realized that I was stepping on four inches of slippery ice. That was when I saw the first person ahead of me fall on their backs with their feet held straight into the air. Then I saw the second one fall. That was when I started to take tiny steps. I did not move my back foot until my front foot was secure on the ice. It took forever for everyone to reach the bus.   The bus driver drove us slowly to the arrival building. For a city of one million inhabitants, the airport was small. When the bus stopped, we exited the bus and walked cautiously inside. The luggage was already inside because the luggage transport did not have to walk on slippery ice, it had arrived quickly.

I grabbed my bags and met my friend and we drove off to the apartment I had rented for my stay. I was exhausted and slept as soon as I had unpacked my suitcases.

The next morning, after eating breakfast we went for a walk. The part of the city where we were walking was located on a high hill. There were no tall buildings or trees and the wind from the steppe bit my face bitterly. I was so cold. At the bottom of the hill, I saw a large river winding through the city. It was completely frozen, making me even colder.

One day, my friend asked if I wanted to go to the circus. One was in town. I had never heard of a circus in the winter. My friend explained to me that Russian circuses were different from American circuses. She explained that they were inside and were based more on ballet, theater, gymnastics, and dance than on anything else. No animals were part of the circus.

I bought tickets to the circus and what followed was the most amazing and entertaining show that I had seen in a long time.

Other than the circus, the city had nothing to see. I was bored and glad that I could only stay a few days.

When it came time to return to Moscow, I refused to take an airplane. I learned that there was an overnight train that went to Moscow. In Russia, all trains go to Moscow. I bought two tickets to Moscow in a suite. It was a two-person cabin with a door that I could lock. Since I did not speak Russian, and not every Russian could be trusted, I was happy to be the only person in my cabin with the door locked.

The train did not depart until late evening. Once we started the trip, a stewardess knocked on the door with two trays of food. It was only a sandwich, an apple, and a cookie, but it was welcome.

I could not see anything out the windows, so I stretched out on the bed and tried to sleep.

That was hard because the train was starting and stopping frequently and rolling gently from side to side. I now understood why it took more than eight hours to travel 350 miles. Finally, I opened my eyes and found that the sun was rising behind a forest of trees. I looked out the window and saw people walking everywhere. I saw several horse-drawn sleighs whizzing by on what appeared to be more than a foot of snow. There were no trees for at least a football field's length and then there was a solid birch tree forest. It was a scene out of the movie "Doctor Zhivago." I sat up and could not stop looking out the window. People were busy walking and riding in sleighs, but I did not see any vehicles.

Soon, I saw a few houses and the forest thinned, and then we were deep into the outskirts of Moscow. From time to time, the train would blow its wailing whistle that always took me back to what I thought would have been during the cold war in a spy movie. Eventually, the train slowed, and I could see that we were approaching the train station. When it stopped, I was nervous because I was in Moscow on my own. I grabbed my suitcase and followed the other passengers leaving the train.

Once outside the train, I saw that we were far from the train station where I was supposed to meet my taxi driver. I started walking and pulling my suitcase. There were so many people walking in both directions that I had to weave my way through them. I kept looking for my taxi driver. Nothing. The train station was still hundreds of feet away. My mind wandered. I thought about what I would do if my taxi driver did not appear. I could only hope that the people who arranged my travel were well organized and did not forget about me or mess up the time or place and that the taxi driver was reliable. After a few minutes of walking, I saw a man standing in the middle of the walkway studying each person as they walked by him. When he saw me, he stopped searching, paused a moment, and walked toward me with a smile and with his hand stretched out to shake my hand. I had met my driver.

After confirming our identities to each other, he reached for my bag and led me to his car. He took me to the airport. I caught my flight and was home in a dozen hours.

Living in Mozambique

One day, I received an invitation from the same Non-Government Organization (NGO) that sent me to Moldova. They asked me to go to Mozambique, Africa. The assignment involved calculating the cost of production of a dozen vegetables grown during the dry season and the rainy season. I also had to estimate the relative risk of growing different crops in both seasons. Plus, I was to study the benefits of the cooperative starting to market their products directly. I accepted the assignment immediately. I had never been to Africa before, but the national language in Mozambique was Portuguese. I could step off the plane speaking the country's official language.

I had to renew my passport, which had to be expedited. When it was not returned to me by the promised date, I learned that it had been stolen and a new one would have to be made. Again, we expedited it. I received it, packed my bags, prepared my camera, and was off to the airport.

My trip would be a 25,000 miles round trip. I flew from St. Louis to Atlanta. In Atlanta, I boarded an evening sixteen-plus-hour flight to Johannesburg, South Africa. After an overnight in Johannesburg, I would fly onward to Beira, Mozambique, a four-hour flight. I was only worried about the sixteen-hour flight from Atlanta to Johannesburg. If I included the time boarding, waiting to take-off, and waiting to de-plane, I could easily be on the plane for more than seventeen hours. Because the NGO always waited until the last moment to buy the ticket, I was usually sitting in the middle seat. That made it difficult to get up to go to the restroom or to stretch my legs, both were especially important activities on such a long flight.

The airplane used for the flight was a Boeing 767. When we boarded the flight, there were no empty seats. The seats were narrow, at least for this fat man. I had trouble putting the meal tray down because my seat and the seat in front of me were so close together, but I managed. What I found difficult was to remain in that position for more than sixteen hours. We took off. Listening to the quiet drone of the engines made me sleepy. I tried to sleep, but I could not. I soon had a headache from being off my normal schedule. I begged the forgiveness of two people and moved into the aisle. I walked back to the galley and asked for water. I prepared my pills and waited for the water. The flight attendant was kind but not elated with the added task of supplying me with water. I took the pills and hung around the bathroom doors and the galley, trying to stretch my legs. This procedure repeated itself a dozen times during the flight.

I tried to watch films, but the headphones would not stay in my ears. I tried to sleep but I could not make myself comfortable. I looked at my watch. Time did not seem to pass.

Eventually, time did pass, and I did survive. We landed. I deplaned. Finally, I was in Johannesburg, Africa. I was exhausted. My trip had started more than twenty hours ago. My flight had crossed ahead about eight time zones. It was late night when I collected my bags and started toward the hotel where I was to stay, which was located at the airport. I had to walk up a ramp to transition from the airport to the hotel. The hotel's Reception was facing me. On a tray were several poured glasses of red wine. I grabbed one and proceeded to the desk. While the receptionist was making my arrangements, I returned and grabbed a second glass of wine. She finished checking me in and gave me my key. I turned and, as I passed the wine, grabbed a third glass. I wanted to sleep quickly because I had an early flight the next morning.

I slept immediately only to have to wake up early. I grabbed my bags and went to the restaurant for breakfast. What a feast! I saw bacon, pork steaks, sausages, fried eggs, scrambled eggs, poached eggs, sliced mangos, pineapple, avocados, and all kinds of other things. I filled my plate twice, but I had to eat fast so I would not miss my flight.

I hurried to pass the security inspection and then on to my gate. The plane arrived and soon the attendant opened the doors and boarding started. I found my seat and situated my carryon and camera. I stood as long as I could in the aisle until I was impeding the aisle traffic. I sat and waited until we took off.

The flight was non-descript, but I was anxious to see Mozambique. What would it be like? Would it remind me of living in Brazil? The name of the city where I was going was Beira. In English that means edge. The city was located on the edge of the ocean. Beira was a small regional city. We landed and I grabbed my luggage and looked for my people. It was easy to find them once I cleared customs.

They took me to their office where they described the purpose of my trip. It was exactly what I had understood. I was introduced to the driver who was to take me across the country to a small city located near the border with Zimbabwe. The drive from Beira was long and hot. It was interesting for me because that was the first time that I was in a vehicle driving in the left-hand lane. Upon arriving in the city, the NGO had rented a house there to receive volunteers. It could shelter three to six volunteers at one time. I was the only occupant when I arrived.

We deposited my baggage in the house and left for a meeting with the committee of my host agencies. They had set up a long table in a storeroom for our meeting. There were hoes and old tires, fertilizer, and other stuff laying around the room. I was nervous as I joined the group.

That first contact was always difficult. After the introductions were made, I asked how they understood my assignment. It coincided with the way I understood it.

The next morning, we were to visit a couple of farms high in the foothills next to the border with Zimbabwe. I returned to my house, took a shower, and thought about eating.

I walked to a place that prepared food and ordered chicken and rice. The restaurant had all its tables outside under a tree with gigantic branch spread. The branches must have hung fifty feet from the trunk in all directions. The trunk itself had a large circumference. There was a breeze making the environment refreshing. Then two monkeys made their appearance. They jumped around the tree and made monkey noises. People started talking and pointing at the monkeys. That was when I noticed that one monkey was carrying a baby dog, a Yellow Labrador. It did not even have its eyes opened yet. The monkeys kept leaping around the branches carrying the little puppy in one hand. Everyone was gasping each time the monkey jumped.

Apparently, a Yellow Labrador had just given birth on the other side of the fence. The monkeys, for whatever reason, darted in and stole one of the puppies. Now people were trying to find a way to reclaim the puppy. The waiter even tried to climb the tree, but the monkeys easily avoided him. I had finished my meal and had to leave. I have always wondered what the puppy's fate was. I hate monkeys.

The next morning, after drinking coffee and eating some French bread, the driver and other members of the group arrived. I grabbed my camera, notepad, and a half-gallon jug of water, and we left. We drove on a highway for half an hour before we pulled into a large village.

The driver went directly to a house and stopped. Out popped the farmer we were about to visit. He was middle-aged and looked like he had spent many days under the sun. His skin was wrinkled, but he had a bright smile. He greeted all of us as he entered our Land Rover.

The driver crossed the highway and drove slowly up a dirt road. It was filled with craters and rocks. It was a bumpy ride until he pulled over to the side of the path and turned off the engine. Everyone left the vehicle. I followed their lead. Someone announced that we had to walk the remaining distance. The owner pointed up the mountain and told us that was our destination. It didn't look too bad.

We climbed and climbed. I was hot and sipped my water. When we looked back, we saw that we had covered a considerable distance, which I judged by the shrinking size of the Land Rover. We kept walking. I was now the last person in the group. I became hotter and hotter as we climbed. My fingers had swollen. I kept sipping on my water. I now wondered if my water would last long enough to get me back to town.

We heard water flowing and started looking around to find it. We found a ditch carved out of the mountain that was one foot wide and two feet deep. It was covered by tall green grass. Water was flowing rapidly straight down the mountain. A member of the group reached down to check what was keeping the ditch from becoming deeper. He found hard clay soil.

We kept walking up the steep slope. Eventually, we reached a man who was hoeing corn. He did not stop his hoeing to look up until the farm owner spoke to him. He was hoeing corn that was eight inches tall. There were stones scattered about the area. From this point, the Land Rover was small. We had an excellent view of the valley below.

To think that corn was planted on this steep slope amazed me. How did they control the soil erosion? We learned that the corn was irrigated. I was curious how they did it without suffering severe soil erosion. The landowner explained that they walked the water down the slope. They introduced the water from the upper left corner of the cornfield. The first row of corn was planted so that it sloped gently down to the end of the row. There, the water dropped to the second row, which was planted such that it dropped a little as it crossed back across the field.

Thusly, they walked the water down the field and avoided soil erosion.

A little more walking took us to the upper border of this gentleman's farm. At the highest point was a hole fifteen feet wide at the top and twenty feet long. At the bottom, it was narrower. It was empty. The landowner explained that high in the mountains was a lake. From the lake water was released into many ditches. Each ditch served a series of farmers as the water flowed down the mountain. As for this farmer, he could capture water once or twice a week to fill his hole. The farmer could then release his stored water whenever he wanted. The hole needed to be large enough to capture enough water to irrigate his crops.

At this point, his water was nearly gone. I started asking the landowner the questions I needed answered so that I could estimate the cost of production. I learned that, due to the steep slope, no vehicle or animal could be used to carry up the seed, fertilizer, or anything else that was needed to produce a crop. It all had to be carried up on men's or women's backs. For the same reason, all products from the farm had to be carried down the mountain on men's or women's backs.

Our work was done. We started down the slope. Walking down the slope was easier, but we still had to be careful because there were loose stones, plus the soil was slippery from constant use. Midway down, I finished my water. Finally, we reached the Land Rover.

We started retracing our steps. When we left the landowner at his home and was on the highway, I asked if there was any place we could buy bottled water. The response was that it was too expensive to be stocked by the local bodegas (small convenience stores). They must have seen how dry I was. Our director asked the driver to pull over at the next bodega. He disappeared into the bodega and a minute later reappeared with a half-gallon of water. I popped the lid and drank whole-heartedly. I was refreshed and happy.

The next day we visited a young farmer's enterprise. He irrigated his crops with a pump by pumping water out of a small pond. He was a very progressive farmer. He had studied agriculture in Zimbabwe at an agricultural high school. He showed us his composting pile. He recycled all weeds that he pulled or crop residue left after harvest. We examined the farmer's black beans production. It looked healthy. The crop did not have a weed in it. Between the rows, the farmer had placed crop residue to minimize water evaporation. He was very efficient. I easily collected his costs of production.

We visited other farms and interviewed other farmers to obtain their costs of production and marketing habits. At night, I worked on the cost of production models that also would give notions of price and production risk. None of the farms were as interesting as the first two farms that we visited.

I had to visit markets to determine the costs of marketing. There was a large market located in one of the small cities. The director took me to the market. I had my camera and clipboard. We went from booth to booth asking questions about how they bought their products and how they sold them. After thirty minutes a well-dressed man approached us and asked us what we were doing. The director explained to him that I was a volunteer working for the farm coop. The man introduced himself as the director of the market. He also informed us that

we could not take photographs or ask questions without a
signed letter of consent from the city

Mayor. The coop director tried to explain what our mission was.
The market director quickly became belligerent and had his
security team escort us from the market. We were left standing
on the street outside the market.

I wore a short-sleeved shirt and felt cold whenever the breeze
blew. We paced back and forth on the sidewalk, not knowing
what to do next. The coop director did not understand the
market director's attitude. After fifteen minutes, the market
director appeared and apologized. He motioned for us to follow
him. He allowed us to wait for the letter from the mayor in an
unused hut. The hut had a dirt floor and a grass roof. It
contained no furniture, so we could not sit while waiting. It was
still cold since the breeze easily penetrated the sticks used for
walls. I wished I had worn a light jacket.

Eventually, the signed permission arrived allowing us to take
photographs and interview the people working in the market. I
quickly obtained enough information to create a market profile.

I presented my results to the coop committee and interested
farmers. I remember one result that was that they should
restrict the area planted to tomatoes in the rainy season
because their costs were elevated, and prices were lower. Just
this recommendation could help all the farmers considerably.
The other recommendations were frosting on the cake.

The trip home was the same. The trip from Johannesburg to
Atlanta was still hard to bear, but I managed.

Living in Angola May 2010

I was excited when I received the invitation from CNFA for a project in Angola, another Portuguese-speaking country in Africa. I obtained my visa and packed my bags. This trip would also be 25,000 miles round-trip. I traveled from St. Louis to Atlanta and then caught a sixteen hour night flight from Atlanta to Johannesburg, South Africa where I spent the night before catching my four-and-a-half-hour flight to Luanda, Angola.

I managed to survive the long flight to Johannesburg. The night in the hotel was as welcome as was the morning's wonderful buffet breakfast. After eating all that I could, I went to the gate to wait for my flight. There I saw many Chinese workmen lounging around on the chairs, while others were sleeping on or underneath them. Still, others were standing around talking and spitting on the floor. I did not understand why so many Chinese were waiting on a flight to Luanda, Angola, especially working-class men.

We boarded the Boeing 747 and took off. As soon as we were at cruising altitude, the Chinese relaxed and again laid on or under the seats to sleep more. This was the only time I heard an announcement in an airplane, "Please, do not lie under the plane's seats." No one moved. I don't think they understood English or Portuguese.

Living in Angola--May 8, 2010

When I exited the plane in Luanda, the heat and humidity were oppressive. I started to sweat immediately. Inside the terminal, I started toward the baggage claim. I was carrying my camera and computer bag. This was a tipoff to everyone that I was "a tourist." As I passed through a doorway, a little man called me from a table set up in a corner. He asked to see my list of vaccinations. He did not speak with confidence and did not bother other people. I had misgivings about him. I handed him the yellow document. After a brief examination, he told me that I lacked the Yellow Fever vaccination. His voice and mannerism were not convincing. I told him that I was there as a volunteer to work in agriculture. He feigned being impressed and repeated that I did not have the required vaccination.

I believed that the little man had picked me from the group to give him a bribe to make the inconvenience of not having a Yellow Fever vaccination go away. I asked how I could correct the oversight and waited for him to suggest something. He never asked for money, but he also never told me what needed to be done. I informed him that one year ago I had been to Mozambique and had received many vaccinations. He repeated that Yellow Fever was missing. I told him my boss was waiting for me in the reception area and he dealt with these matters daily and would know. I asked permission to go to bring him back to discuss it with the little man. The little man gave up and told me to go tell my boss to do something to overcome the problem before returning. He had given up.

I found my bag and walked toward the street. The door opened and a crowd of people waiting in the reception area for family and friends appeared. Among them was a young lady, maybe eighteen years old, with my name on a sign. I smiled and we walked outside. She was dressed nicely in blue jeans and a green sweater. Her hair was neatly done. She told me that no taxis were currently available. She made many phone calls. People were continuously exiting the airport and finding cars and leaving, but no taxi appeared.

Between phone calls, Bebo, the name of the young lady, explained to me how she had been assaulted that morning while she walked from her home to a bus stop. The would-be thief cut the strap to her purse and in the process nicked her arm. She was able to hang onto the purse and the two cell phones she was carrying: hers and what was to be mine. It was evident that she was shaken by the experience.

After an hour, a young man approached smiling. He had answered Bebo's plea for help and came to our rescue. We drove to the hotel. Bebo and he were talking as we traveled. I believed their acquaintance was deeper than that between a driver and a client. But mostly, I observed. I noticed the city was very dirty, more so than cities in Moldova, Ukraine, and even in Mozambique. Trash was everywhere. I also noticed that street vendors were moving into their positions pushing wheelbarrows and carrying their goods and wares. Traffic was undisciplined, but without many horns honking. Tall apartment buildings were old and unkept with faded paint and people's laundry drying on a line secured outside their windows. This gave the buildings a look of cheapness.

Suddenly, the driver turned into a narrow passage in the middle of a nondescript street and followed the path behind a small building. This was my hotel. It was a small two-story building with no signs. It was not a Ramada Inn. We carried my bags inside. They asked me to sit at a patio table in an open area. Bebo said we would wait more because no one had yet arrived to sign me into the hotel. We waited for an hour before she disappeared and returned. Now, she explained that check-in was at noon; however, knowing that I was tired, hot, and sweaty from my thirty hours of flying and hanging around airports, they assigned me a room temporarily until a single room became available later. I could not sleep because if I slept, I would not be able to awake in three or four hours. Bebo asked for my passport because she had to buy my airline passage to Huambo the next morning. Huambo was my destination in the middle of Angola.

I closed the door and looked for the shower. It was hot inside the room. I turned on the air conditioner. To further cool off, I washed my hair thoroughly and then removed the sweat before soaking it a bit. After showering, I lay down on the bed and stretched in all directions.

As I lay, I listened to the sounds. I heard people talking. Some were near while others were more distant. Some conversations were loud and then faded. Some were one-sided-perhaps, they were on the telephone. I heard chairs moving, pots clanging, cars honking and braking, and then accelerating, and all sorts of sirens. The sirens came in a variety of bursts and degrees of loudness. I had no idea what they were. The sounds were all different from American sirens.

Also, I heard jackhammers and pigeons. It was not a quiet zone.

Later, I answered the phone and was notified that it was time to move to another room. Once in my new room, I tried to sleep again, then Bebo appeared. She handed me the airline ticket and said that the driver was to come by at 9:00 that evening to take my check-in luggage to the airline and check it in for tomorrow morning's flight. We had to be back at the airport at 5:00

a.m. tomorrow morning to catch the plane.

I did some calculations. I did not want to sleep too much so that I could not sleep at night.

I decided not to take my sleeping pills until just before giving my luggage to the driver at 9:00

p.m. I laid down to rest. After a couple hours, I found I could not sleep, so I decided it was time to go for a walk. For safety reasons, I did not take my camera and only enough money to exchange one-hundred dollars. I needed to buy something to eat for the afternoon and night.

I looked for a place to buy some inexpensive food. I walked blocks and saw nothing. I noticed that there were no restaurants, no bars, and no places to eat a snack. There were few stores open. I saw one attractive, but small store. It sold kitchen items. The store was no more than fifteen feet wide. Next to it was a vacant store, without windows. The smell signaled that people used it as a restroom. Finally, I found a small crowded market. I pushed my way in. I saw nothing of interest except two liters of peach juice and a box of cookies. My bill was eleven dollars. I went home, happy.

At 8:30 p.m. the driver arrived to take my bag to the airport, except that I had misunderstood. I also had to go. Thirty minutes prior I had taken my sleeping pills hoping to sleep well before my flight. I dressed quickly and we went to the pickup. It was parked in the back of the building, trapped by another vehicle. We waited for twenty minutes before someone sleepily came out and moved the car so we could leave.

At the airport, I was surprised to see a large crowd. I did not expect many people. I was directed to stand in line, but there was no line, only a mass of people. People were pushing and shoving, even though no one knew which door would open. Finally, they let one or two airline employees in, and the pushing started in earnest. Then another and another employee entered.

After a few minutes, they opened the gate and the mob rushed into a large room.

Inside, people started another line. It grew in length and width as people began cutting inline ahead of other people. Then people cut in on the people who had just cut in. I noticed that no one was processing people. Employees were standing there but they were doing nothing. My sleeping pill was starting to work its magic.

Finally, my driver made his way into the room. He pulled me out of line to tell me the flight had been cancelled. Then, the employees placed four signs, each with a different destination. The big line quickly realigned itself according to the four destinations. There were three other flights, besides mine. Still, no one was processed.

People not only had luggage, but they also had boxes, cases, and packages of all sizes, shapes, and weights. It was difficult to stand in line without falling over someone's box, case, or package. The driver tried to obtain more information about the flight. At first, the flight was cancelled and then it was not, and then it again was. No one knew. Finally, a few people started to be processed into another long line. I had no idea for which flight or flights they were for. A military man appeared. I thought he was going to help keep order, but he cut into line ahead of me.

After more than an hour, the driver told me to follow him. We walked outside and continued for another 200 yards. We entered an office to have my flight changed to the next day. Even they did not know that my flight had been cancelled; although, the other flights were still scheduled. It took an additional thirty minutes for them to understand that my flight was cancelled. We made the reservation quickly and returned home. I was asleep immediately.

Living in Angola--May 9, 2010

When I awoke, I went into the restaurant area where there was a free breakfast. It consisted of peach juice, French bread, ham, and cheese. I stuffed myself. The price of my room was 160 dollars per day. It was a small and modest room. It had a shower with hot water. The TV captured one boring channel. The room had an air conditioner, but it struggled to keep the room cool. It was all that I needed, but I could not help but be surprised by the 160-dollar price tag.

Since there was nothing for me to do until that evening, to kill time, I walked around the city and found it distressingly simple. I saw no fast-food places; although, I believed this was positive; it was also a sign of the region's lack of purchasing power. I noticed that, on some apartment buildings, iron bars were placed on windows up to the sixth floor. I considered this an index for public safety. If people living on the sixth floor did not feel safe, then the city was not likely safe.

I visited a bakery and bought some sweet rolls to eat at night and in the morning before I went to the airport. I noticed that all soda cans were placed upside down in the display case. I asked why. The lady was surprised that I had to ask. She said it was to keep the top of the can clean until it was opened.

Tonight, within the hour, I would make my second trip to the airport. I was nervous but ready. I had eaten and hydrated. I had not taken sleeping pills and had a bottle of water with headache pills ready. I was ready for whatever might come.

When the driver arrived, I was ready but nervous. I did not look forward to participating in another stampede at the airport. Upon arriving at the airport, I left the truck and "entered the line" somewhere in the middle. It was approximately ten feet long and twenty feet wide. People were relaxed and spread out; most were talking happily. One woman stood out. She was short and wide and had a harsh voice that carried far. I am sure she could be heard a mile away. It became obvious that she commanded the area with her voice.

People continued to arrive. Little by little the crowded area became more compact. Two guards appeared and stood in front of the people by the door. People pressed closer as more moved into more favorable positions. When two more guards appeared and opened the two doors, people became excited and surged forward. They were stopped by the guards, who were now yelling for the people to remain calm. I was being compressed and my feet barely touched the ground. That was when they popped open the barrier that separated us from the airport terminal. There was a surge forward. My upper torso was tossed forward, but without any support from my feet to follow. For a second, I thought I was going down. Finally, my feet connected with the floor and I raced with the others inside.

Two women with packages were moving briskly, but they lost their footing on the corner and fell to the floor. Their feet never stopped moving. When their hands steadied themselves, they were up and maintained their place in the line. Within seconds, the mass of people had moved from outside to inside, but it was still an unorganized mass. People were already cutting in front of me and I was within five feet from the front of the line. They cut in on the left and on the right. They came in low, squeezed between people, and lifted themselves up like they had been there all along.

The workers behind the stand braced themselves against the stand to keep it from being pushed. We were unable to keep from moving forward as people pushed against us. Minutes passed and nothing happened except more pushing from all sides. Fifteen minutes passed before they brought out the four signs indicating the four destinations for different flights. They were placed close together. The people quickly started to realign themselves according to their destinations. The line was again ten feet wide as these four lines merged into one wide line with people still cutting in on all sides.

Suddenly, the airline employees started looking at papers and waving people to the next line. It was unclear if they were processing people for all flights or for one specific flight. No announcements were made. No announcements were ever made. People pushed and yelled and protested about others who had cut in front of them. The workers did what they could, but that was nothing. People were being waved into the next line where they had their luggage checked.

That was the last line, and everyone wanted to be in it.

While the employee checked the documentation at the counter, two or three people rushed the cord and ducked under it, and ran directly to the final line. Other people protested until the worker looked up and ordered the intruders back on the other side of the barricade. While he was doing this, two or three people ducked under the barricade on the other side and made their run to the final line. The process repeated many times. Sometimes the employee was able to process one or two people legally before he had to bring back the illegal barricade jumpers.

Finally, it was my turn. I could not believe it. I took twenty steps forward with my luggage. Within a few minutes, my luggage was checked, and I left the building looking for my driver. I was happy as we drove back to the hotel. All this hassle was to check the luggage.

I was excited about seeing the interior of Angola the next day. I took a shower after sweating in the airport, checked all my carry-on items, and set my alarm clock. I tried to sleep, but it was slow to come.

Living in Angola--May 10, 2010

I awoke before 5:00 a.m. I gobbled the two sweet rolls that I had previously purchased and rushed to pack. At 5:20 a.m. the driver knocked on my door and we left. The streets were empty making our drive to the airport unimpeded. We arrived at the airport at 5:45 a.m. The driver stopped on the street outside the terminal, and I got out of the truck and was on my own. I crossed the street and walked past the guards across the parking lot and into the airport terminal.

The entrance was not blocked by guards as it had been the previous night. I walked in and passed through the inspection. I entered the waiting area, which was already full of people.

My flight was to leave by 6:30 a.m. A bus arrived and people lined up, sort of, and had their documents checked before entering the bus. I asked a service agent if that was my flight. It was not. In fact, I asked him the same question every five minutes. Finally, he told me to sit down in front of him and he would tell me when to board the bus. After all the difficulty obtaining my ticket and checking my luggage, I did not want to miss the bus that took me from the airport to the plane.

The airport was warm, even in the early morning. I did not sweat, but one degree warmer and I would have.

Finally, the service agent motioned for me to come. I did and entered the bus parked nearby. Within a few minutes, we departed in the direction of the airplanes. Most airplanes I saw had propellers. I hoped that none of them would be mine. Finally, we stopped in front of a Boeing 737 aircraft. The luggage we had fought to check-in the previous night was laid out on the tarmac in front of the aircraft. At first, I did not understand, but finally, I understood that we had to identify our luggage and load it onto a cart, or it would not be loaded onto the aircraft.

I found a seat and made myself comfortable. The plane was very cold. We departed soon after with only a few people on board. We were all cold and reached around to turn off as many air vents as we could, but the temperature remained cold.

I heard an argument in the aisle behind me. I did not see what started it, but it was between a steward and a twenty-year-old male passenger. From the passenger's behavior, I believe alcohol was involved. After the steward's stern words, the passenger returned to his seat and slept.

Eventually, we started our descent into Huambo. The ride was rough. Suddenly and unexpectedly, the pilot pushed the throttle forward and the airplane creaked as it started to climb quickly. The first thought that came to mind was that a mountain had appeared. He made a turn and continued to climb. The pilot then made an announcement, but no one could understand due to the static. Finally, the steward went to the pilot's cabin and asked. When he returned, he told us that the weather was unfavorable in Huambo and we were returning to Luanda to await better weather.

I was disappointed. After all, we had gone through to get on the flight. I did not want to have to repeat it. The airplane was still very cold. Upon landing, we were bused to the airport and told to wait. The airport was now hot, and I began to sweat.

I found other passengers who had been in the airplane and sat in the middle of them. A few hours passed, and finally, we were called back to the bus and then back to the airplane. I had to re-identify my luggage. This time, the plane was full but still cold. I could feel my throat and my head starting to hurt. I was feeling tired.

Upon nearing Huambo, the plane descended and landed. The airport was small and simple. The plane parked away from the terminal. We went through the customs check and waited for our baggage. There was no belt, only a concrete slab to pile the luggage on. The airline workers carried the bags into a small room. The first object brought in was a huge pistol. It was claimed by the young man who appeared intoxicated on the plane.

After a few minutes, I found my bag and left the terminal. Once outside, I saw the people waiting for me. After exchanging greetings, we found the vehicle and loaded my things into it. We went to my hotel where I checked in and paid in advance. I went to my room to leave my luggage. The room had a bad smell to it. I tried to identify it, but I could not.

We immediately went to a restaurant to eat. They had a buffet. I ate a few things and paid twenty dollars. Against my will, we went to the city's zoo. I only wanted to return to my hotel room to rest. We paid ten dollars to enter the zoo's gate. It had nothing of interest to me, but we had to walk around for thirty minutes for the other group members' benefit. I took no photographs. One person said that the zoo had been better in years past, but many of the animals had disappeared. He thought the people had climbed over the fence and killed them to eat.

I felt a bad cold coming. After being exposed to heat and cold so many times that morning, I was not surprised at my feeling tired and feverish.

We went to a park where there were many statues of the city's Founding Fathers and their wives. I noticed holes in all of them and thought they had rusted through. Then, our guide said that those were bullet holes from the fighting that occurred during the twenty-five-year civil war.

I took some photographs.

We drove into the country and found a small lake that our guides wanted to show us. It was nice, but my body was hurting from the cold coming on and from the journey. We drove around the lake and to the far side. Every foot had a bump and my body felt like it was being beaten with a stick. Finally, I thought we could just continue a little to exit the park, but we had to retrace our steps, bump by bump.

By 4:00 p.m., I returned to my hotel. I took a shower and slept. Late that night I awoke with a terrible hunger, but there was nothing to eat. My head hurt. I took aspirin and tried to sleep, but I could not. My headache and hunger kept me awake.

At 6:00 a.m. I went downstairs hoping for breakfast. There was nothing. I waited and even at 6:30, there was nothing. I thought I was going to die. I went back upstairs to my room and took more aspirins and returned. Finally, at 7:00 a.m., French bread was placed on the table with instant coffee.

The driver and agronomist came by the hotel and picked me up. We went to visit one of two brothers with whom CNFA had been working. This farmer had a large farm, most of which he did not farm for lack of capital. He had two large tractors and a plow he used to break up the grass sod. The native grass was more than six feet tall, especially when the dozens of acres were not grazed by more than a couple of oxen. The grassland generated no revenue nor benefit other than resting the soil.

When he showed me the potatoes, I could not see them for the tall weeds that encompassed them. We went to a spot where a half dozen women with babies strapped to their backs were digging them. When I saw the potatoes, I noticed how small they were. I also noticed that there were large gaps in the rows of plants. There were twenty-foot strips without a single potato plant. He bragged that he was obtaining three tons per acre. He should be able to obtain twenty tons per acre. I was not impressed. I learned that he was saving seeds from his own crop to plant the next crop. This seed was likely infested with viruses that inhibited the yield.

The farmer was limited in how many acres he could plant because he farmed only the area that he could self-finance. He did not borrow money from any bank because the interest rates were high. That was why he reuse his seed; he saved money on seed and could plant more acres. He considered the quantity of acres more important than its quality.

Water was pumped from high on the farm into a clay ditch that ran down the slope. The ditch was not dug mechanically but by water erosion. The hard clay kept it from becoming deeper. Every hundred feet or so along the ditch, a slot was carved into the dirt allowing some water to escape the ditch and drain onto the field. There, a bunch of men was leaning on their shovels. Their job was to dig the water across the rows to allow it to run to the low end of the field. This was necessary because they did not plant on the contour.

From this farm, we stopped by a huge outdoor market on our way back to Huambo. It occupied more than a half-mile by a half-mile. It was huge. In this market, one could buy meat, vegetables, stoves, refrigerators, CDs, clothes, pickups, semi-trucks, trailers, furniture, electronic goods, and spare parts. You could find anything in this market. It was located on bare ground.

Whenever the wind blew, dust blew everywhere.

We went to the meat market, which consisted of a series of stands arranged in a large rectangle. Along the outer edge were individual stands where women competed to sell different cuts and types of meat. The meat was hanging on hooks and laying on the counter. Flies were everywhere. In the center, on the ground, were a few cardboard boxes laid out flat with a quarter of beef laying on it. A barefoot teenager was standing on the beef to stabilize it while he swung an ax to divide the quarter into smaller pieces. The cardboard had dirt on it in addition to the meat. I never again ate beef in Angola.

When I had seen enough of the market, we returned to my hotel. As we approached, I saw a huge tank truck in front unloading. It appeared like a fuel truck that was unloading at a gas station. I asked what it was. It was the hotel stocking up on water. The city's water was often unreliable and off-line. To keep its guests happy, they had to always have a large inventory of freshwater, which they trucked in.

The truck was parked next to a huge generator. The source of electricity was even less reliable than water was. Electricity could be off-line for days at a time. When I looked around, I noticed that all businesses had an electric generator. Even CNFA had a diesel generator located in the backyard for its office; although I was told that it was broken.

We went to a restaurant that offered a buffet. They offered beef, pork, chicken, rice, white beans, and other dishes. I ate chicken, rice, and beans. It cost thirty dollars.

In the afternoon, we went to visit a women's coop. There were a dozen members, each owning a dozen or so acres, most of which were not farmed due to lack of capital. The women were very gracious and grateful that we were trying to help them. I felt a strong desire to help these modest women who were attempting to grub a living for their families from the land. By the time we returned to my hotel, the evening meal was done. This meant that no food was left-over, and I could not eat. At my insistence, they admitted that they had some rice leftover. I asked them to reheat the rice and fry a couple of eggs. They granted me my wish. My bill was seventeen dollars. I paid my bill and added three cold Cokes to it. I took the Cokes to my room and placed them in my refrigerator to keep them cold for consumption during the night if I should become hungry.

The next morning, we left to visit the other brother's farm. It was not located on the main highway. We had to leave the main highway and travel down a dirt road filled with questionable bridges. The driver always slowed and crawled over each of these bridges made from loose planks. Later, the road narrowed, and we turned from it onto a vehicle path. We proceeded at a snail's pace because the road was filled with ruts and was very rough. We were bouncing all over the cab and had to take care not to hit our heads on the roof.

It took forty-five minutes to travel a few miles. We met the landowner at the farm. He proudly showed me around. After I had seen his farm, he answered my questions concerning his costs of production. He seemed to be more progressive than his brother. His potato rows were closer to being on the contour, thusly, easier to irrigate.

After collecting data on the farmer's costs of production, we returned to the office to work on the Excel spreadsheet that I would use to present my results to the farmers.   The next day we traveled in the opposite direction from Huambo to visit a large agricultural coop. We met the directors who discussed their operation. The coop had suffered several setbacks and was near bankruptcy. From what I understood, there was little that we could do to save the coop. We decided to look at it anyway.

We traveled a few miles down the road before we turned into grasslands to follow a vehicle path. As far as we could see there was grass taller than the pickup. After a few miles of turning this way and then that way, we located a small building that was the coop's farm building. We stopped and were greeted by their farm manager. He climbed into the pickup and showed us their failed corn crop. The mature stalks were sparse, thin, and with no ears. The field even contained few weeds. The sandy ground was mostly barren. It seemed to me that corn was a poor choice of crops for dry land farming on sandy soil where rain was sparse and unreliable.

The farm manager then showed us their cassava planting. The plants were not as large as I would like to have seen, but the roots were medium-sized. This was a fantastic result considering the dry year they had. It seemed to me that cassava may have been more appropriate for the soil than corn was.

I noticed that acres and acres of tall grass were left unharvest. This may have built the soil, but it seemed to me that they could have fenced the area and bought cattle to graze the grass using rotational grazing. Any grass that grew too much for the cattle to graze could have been cut and placed on the compost pile. The compost could then be used to aid in producing a small acreage of some high-value crop such as potatoes or tomatoes.

I learned that many Chinese workers were Chinese prisoners. Instead of paying to house them in Chinese prisons, they formed a government agency and did construction work outside the country. They were in many African countries where they built docks, railroads, airports, roads, and even farmhouses. All resources used were Chinese. They used Chinese cement, trucks, bulldozers, cranes, everything was Chinese. This increased the demand for these products in China, thus stimulating their economy. The workers only earned modest wages, thus increasing China's capture of foreign currencies. For China, it was a win-win process.

I prepared my results from my trip and personally presented them to each of my hosts: the two farmers, the ladies' coop, and the large coop. My recommendations were:

1.   Plant fewer acres of potatoes but use the saved capital for buying inspected potato seed and use more fertilizer.

2.   Plant on the contour and then irrigate down the row. Labor could be saved, and irrigation could be more effective.

3.   Buy as many milk cows, sheep, or goats as you could. Fence in small areas, each area should be large enough for the animals to graze no more than three days; then move the animals to another paddock. When the first paddock had regrown enough that it had juicy leaves and enough that it could replace the energy sacrificed by the roots to restart the plant growing, it could be grazed again.

4.   Cut the remaining grass. Collect the stalks and start to compost it.

5.   Use the compost to grow some high-value crop, such as tomatoes, or other vegetables.

My return trip to St. Louis was uneventful.

Living in Angola—May, 2011

My flight from the USA to Johannesburg was no eventful as was the flight on to Luanda. I spent my day in Luanda walking around and at night I made my trip to the airport to check-in. I was used to the chaos, so it did not bother me. There was one difference. Instead of buying a ticket to

Huambo, I bought one to Kuito, a smaller regional city about two hours by car east from Huambo. The Huambo airport was under modernization and could not be used for several months.

I said goodbye to the driver in Luanda and went through customs. Basically, that consisted of walking through a door and finding a chair to sit down. I drank two café lattes and sat to wait. The waiting room filled. There were many children. Finally, the plane arrived. After twenty minutes, it made its way to the gate and slowly, very slowly, started to disembark its passengers.

People inside the airport started to stand and press towards the door. It was another uncontrolled crowd. Airline employees went through the door to stand outside the terminal. A group of employees accumulated outside. They talked and laughed mostly. Then, some would come back inside. This continued for about an hour, and then a female employee walked from the plane towards us as she chewed on a piece of sugar cane stalk which she spits out every few steps. She cracked the door and whispered something to another employee and then closed it and walked away.

Someone understood what she had said and interpreted for the rest of us. The plane had a small technical difficulty. Everyone turned and rushed to claim a favorably placed chair in the waiting room. After another hour they called us. They opened the door and we burst forth. We walked quickly to the baggage which was spread out on the tarmac in front of the plane. Each passenger had to find his or her baggage and physically place it on the baggage cart. Then, they loaded it on the plane. Why? I do not know. I wondered how that system worked during the rainy season.

After a one-hour flight, we arrived in Kuito. Claiming my luggage was easy. It was laid out on a concrete slab. All we had to do was point and our luggage was handed to us.

I walked outside and found my driver waiting. We had an uneventful drive to Huambo.

When I arrived in Huambo, after three full days of travel, I learned that I was scheduled to give a statistics course at the university the next day for the university's instructors and agricultural extension agents. I was shocked because I wrote the Scope of Work myself, and that was not part of it. I tried to keep myself calm and remind myself that I needed to serve the country's needs, and if they changed since our last meeting, then I would also need to change.

The university class started at 9:00 a.m. I arrived at the university and found the classroom, except it was locked. I waited for the first professor to arrive and asked him about the key. He went about finding it. Meanwhile, other instructors and Extension Agents arrived and waited with me. One or two others decided to also look for the key and departed.

By 10:00 a.m. a key was found, and we entered the classroom. It was a huge computer classroom. It had tile floors, concrete walls, and a wooden ceiling. I looked for a chalkboard and found one that was three by four feet. It was not large enough for my needs, even so, it had no chalk. I kept looking and found a whiteboard, but it was also small and had no markers. Another instructor left to find markers so I could use the whiteboard while another left to find chalk for the chalkboard. I was unable to start class until 10:30 a.m.

I discovered immediately that there was a significant echo in the room. If I spoke continuously, I confused myself because there was a strong and constant echo. It bothered me but did not seem to bother anyone else. They were used to it. My remedy was to talk for three seconds, then pause a few seconds until the echo receded, and then I spoke for another three seconds. It was unsettling for me.

Midway through the lecture, a professor's cell phone rang. He fumbled around to find it and then answered it. He spoke loudly. It caused me to pause the lecture. I had hoped that he would walk toward the door and talk outside. He did not. Finally, I asked him to take his call outside. He did not respond. I had to ask a second time. He looked like I had hurt his feelings and was angry at the same time. I now know that I should have paused the class and allowed him to finish his conversation. By doing so, I would not have challenged his authority. He was a person of authority in the institution and was not accustomed to people telling him what to do. I committed an error in judgment.

People were always entering and exiting the classroom. Few remained in the classroom during the entire class period. It was hard to develop a flow in learning since almost everyone had missed a part of the lecture. It was very distracting, but none of the professors and instructors seemed to mind.

For an exercise in how to find the sample size needed to estimate a parameter to within a certain range, we went to one of the experimental station's cassava plantings located next to our classroom. We estimated the plant population and distance between plants. The participants seemed to enjoy the exercise and were surprised by the results.

The last day of my class in the College of Agriculture arrived. In Angola, such a class cannot end without a closing ceremony, even if it included only a few hours of instruction. We went to the auditorium with the graduation certificates. The press was there. The head table was full of people, almost more than sat in the auditorium. I and three other people alternated in handing out the certificates, holding the handshake for the photo, and the student giving a sign of victory, even if no exams were given. I noticed that all the students I handed the certificates to were men with beards. The head dude handed the certificates to the ladies. No handshake was involved for him, but three kisses to the check. That was not even a little fair.

While on campus I asked to see the university library. I could not believe my eyes. The entire library was not as large as my personal library. I loved books and spent thousands of dollars on books, but this was still ridiculous. The students had no books. The professors had no books. The library had no books. They all have been dealt a difficult hand to play.

We returned to the CNFA office to finish the paperwork. I had to account for every penny spent and generate a report for all my achievements. It was not long. A professor from the university came to visit me. He had given me research data and wanted assistance in setting it up for analysis. I spent about two hours with him showing him how he should proceed. I could see the lights go on as he watched me manipulate the data.

Living in Angola--May 11, 2011

I was up early and drank my peach nectar. This was my only breakfast. We prepared my stuff and we headed to a distant farm. We traveled thirty minutes on the highway, but our average speed was not great since the traffic was complicated. People were walking, especially children going to and from school. There were also adults and children carrying things, such as an empty plastic container (one to five gallons) to fetch water. Motorcycles were carrying as many as four people plus merchandise. Minibuses were darting in and out to pick up and drop off people.

There were also trucks of all sizes hurrying about.

Living in Angola--May 12, 2011

Yesterday morning, there was no water when I tried to shower. No problem. We had a twenty gallon bucket for such occasions; however, it was not heated so my bath was with cold water. Also, yesterday at about noon there was no electricity. Our offices were dark, but we could still work. We always kept our laptops charged, so, if we were careful, we could continue our work. For me, however, the problem was that this produced eye strain, and I had a severe headache all afternoon and night. I spent much of the night trying to sleep sitting up.

The agronomist and I worked on crop budgets. This seemed straightforward, but it was like pulling teeth. In part, it was the language; although I was fluent in Portuguese; it was Brazilian Portuguese. Many words were not the same in Portuguese Portuguese. Occasionally, the terms were the same, but the pronunciation was different. The largest problem was that we thought differently. In the end, we made progress.

At 10:00 a.m., I went to a small grocery store. They had cookies, and I was hungry. Usually, there was a young lady who worked there. She was always helpful. Today, she was not there. A young man was working, and he had his friends in the store. One stood in the middle of the doorway and did not move. I excused myself and asked permission to enter the store. It seemed like I was creating a major inconvenience to the young men, so I turned and left the store.

Around the corner, there was a larger market. It even had a generator on the sidewalk that was as large as a car, only taller. I entered this store. The first thing I noticed was that nearly twenty-five percent of the shelf space was empty, and the rest was poorly stocked. I looked for cookies. I found that the selection was limited. What they did have was in large package sizes that I would never buy. It had no fruits, no vegetables. Its freezers and coolers were empty. I bought a small package of cookies and left.

At noon, I went to a small local restaurant to eat. I was starving. Here, they prepared a small buffet, but my experience was that it would be ready at 12:00 and by 1:00 p.m., if you had not eaten, the selection would be poor or there would be nothing at all to eat. This time, only the soup was ready. I asked when the rest would be ready. The boy replied, "Soon," but I noticed he was annoyed that I would ask. I pressed the issue. He said he did not know. I asked again, giving him a multiple-choice, five minutes, ten minutes, fifteen minutes, or more. He answered fifteen minutes.

After more waiting, he announced that the soup was ready, I grabbed the soup bowl and filled it to its brim. Its cost was three dollars. I sat and ate it as fast as I could because I was starving. No one came to ask me if I wanted to drink anything.

A man was seated at the table in front of me. He ordered a beer. The boy took him a beer, almost forgetting to open it. The boy was watching a Brazilian soap opera and walked to the table as he watched the TV. The man, already annoyed, asked the boy for a glass. Now, the boy was also annoyed. He grabbed a glass and gave it to the man. From my table, I saw that the glass was extremely dirty, maybe never washed. The man asked for another glass. The boy, never taking his eyes from the TV answered that they didn't have any more glasses. The man started pouring his beer into the glass and almost immediately it started foaming. Most of the beer he poured into the glass foamed and ended up on the table. The man again asked for another glass. The boy, eyes fixed on the TV, again replied no. The man grabbed a napkin and whipped the bottle mouth and drank the beer from the bottle. I finished my soup, paid, and left.

Upon returning to the office, I asked for them to take me to a store that sells agricultural machinery and other inputs since there was still no electricity. We drove to the outskirts of the city and turned into a place that sold tractors and implements. It was closed. A guard came, cracked the gate, and said that they were not open. The owner was in Luanda (400 miles away) and he didn't know when the owner would return. This was a large place. They had many tractors in inventory plus implements, yet it was closed.

We went to another place. They were closed but would reopen at 2:30 p.m. It was now just 1:00 p.m. We could not wait. The agronomist called another place. They were closed and would open at 3:00 p.m.

We returned to the dark office and tried to continue our work. My head was aching, and I did not achieve much. At 3:00 p.m., we went to the store where we waited another twenty minutes for the man to arrive. He had a large store, but in it, he only had one small tractor, one four-row corn planter, and a few sacks of fertilizer.

We went to his office to talk. I started explaining what I wanted. He said he could not give me prices without a lot of work. If I would make a list of the items I wanted to price, when he had time, he would look them up in his files. I knew that would never happen. We exchanged pleasantries and left.

My head was killing me. I laid down. It was almost dark. The office closed and I was left alone. There was no electricity, so I laid down. I did not get up again until morning.

Living in Angola--May 14, 2011

Yesterday we went to the university campus. The trip to the university was pleasant. Nearly ninety percent of the road was paved compared to half of that last May. They were working on the other ten percent. Progress was occurring. I met with the state Director of the

Agricultural Experimental Station. He had a Ph.D. from Cornell University and was a good man. I was surprised; yet, sad to discover how much he depended on our help. They had almost nothing to work with except their own goodwill. I gave him two technical books that he could use as he saw fit. He was pleased. He informed me that he desperately needed statistics books on the introductory level, analysis of variance, and linear regression. I promised that, when I returned in August, I would bring as many books as I could.

Part of my problem was that everyone needed books. The Angolan Director of CNFA wanted Math books. The agronomist who helped me so much needed more books and the educator that also helps me needed books in economics, statistics, and management. Books were heavy. I envisioned these books would weigh one hundred pounds or more.

As the Director and I spoke, a German lady joined us. She had a Ph.D. in botany and worked with potatoes. I had met her last May. She was so competent that it made me feel bad compared to her. She was an asset that I needed to use more. What a lady! At the end of our meeting, he invited me to give another statistics course in August. I left the meeting very energized. I only hoped that I could follow through and help bring these technical people the resources they needed to do their job.

On the way back to the CNFA office, I asked my colleague what an inexpensive house would cost to rent in Huambo. He replied that it would be from $1,500 to $3,000 a month. After emphasizing that I wanted only the minimum, not a luxurious house, replied that, maybe, $1,500 would do.

In most restaurants, a plate of food costs from fifteen to twenty dollars plus a couple dollars for drinks and a couple dollars for a tip. This meal consisted of a cup of rice, French fries, a small salad, a sauce plus potatoes, meat, cabbage, and a piece of meat or fish. The sauce was good to mix in with the rice.

I was given fifty dollars a day to pay for my food and personal expenses. I ate one meal in a restaurant each day. I usually had fruit juice and cookies for breakfast. My favorite juice was cashew. I loved it. I must return to the supermarket tomorrow and buy several liters. I had not had any for a couple days. One liter of this juice and one small box of cookies cost six dollars. For supper, I ate the same thing that I ate for breakfast. Doing this, I spent about forty dollars a day on food. My diet there was simple.

I worked with three people: a driver, an educator, and an agronomist. They were all excellent professionals and were highly competent in their jobs. They often did not eat lunch. I assumed they ate breakfast, but they seldom stopped for lunch. Often, we were traveling in a rural area visiting farms, farmers, or coops. In these areas, there was no reliable place to eat. Even stopping to buy water or soda was expensive, more so than in the cities, because it must be transported from the city out to the rural area. The merchandise often had been there a long time.

The local population could not afford it.

The educator attended the university at night to study management. His classes went from 6:00 to 11:30 p.m. He maybe had time to stop by his home to eat something before he went to class. He was always at work before 8:00 a.m. He was married and had four children. He came to the office on Saturday mornings to study for a few hours. Sunday was for his family and church.

All three of my colleagues were excellent men. They did not drink nor did they smoke. They were married with as many as nine children. They were religious and attended church regularly. They did not seem to enjoy my jokes; however, I kept trying to make them laugh.

Living in Angola--May 16, 2011

It was 2:00 a.m. and I could not sleep. A dog barked constantly, but there was no yelling, no parties, and no traffic. I went to bed at 6:00 p.m. because we had no electricity and there was nothing to do. I had read a book on the front porch, which was where I could capture the most light. When it was too dark to read, there was nothing else to do but to go to bed.

I placed the mosquito spray on my bed stand after spraying a few seconds around the room. The window was closed, and I closed the door to isolate myself as much as possible. Even so, the night was punctuated with buzzzzz....swat...buzzzz.... swat, spray, peace. And then, the process was repeated.

The weekend was spent working on my farm budget computer program to finish it, or to make it usable for my presentation on Wednesday. During the last fifteen months, I had spent hundreds of hours teaching myself to program in VBA-Excel, and now, I was becoming productive. A difficult part of this was to obtain accurate data for the individual operations used in the production process. We had land preparation using tractor and disc, oxen and wooden plow, and by hand. Likewise, there were a host of other variations. These must be accurately described before any budgeting program could do its work. Estimating the cost of production was not a simple task.

I was becoming accustomed to it now, but it had taken many mental exercises to obtain accurate data. For example, I asked how many man-days did it take to hand cultivate potatoes.

They told me that men do not do this, only women do it. Then they said twenty-five man-days. As I started to enter the data, they said, "No, wait, it's ten man-days." Again, before I could enter the data, it was "No, put forty man-days." Now, which number should I use? The people were providing me with the best information they had. The problem was that no one had paid attention to this before and no one really knew.

Part of my recommendations involved the collection of data. I developed forms they would need to collect the data. The process of introducing these forms, selecting the people who must fill them in daily, and convince them they must do it every day was imperative. Each person would need to be supervised each day for many weeks, if not months before reliable data could be obtained. The form itself would undergo many modifications during this process.

In conjunction with this, I needed to develop a computer program to allow people to enter the data that would generate reports. This suggested that the coops and large farmers must buy computers, the program Excel, and obtain trained people to operate them. This was part of the economic development process. I must obtain books on Excel in English (I cannot find any in Portuguese) and bring them to Angola. Another possibility was to enhance my "tutorials" for Excel that I have developed for my students at Southern Illinois University Edwardsville. Once perfected, they would need to be translated into Portuguese.

Today we visited a coop to collect data from invoices. Several farmers, ladies, and the large coop were supposed to have all their invoices ready for me to arrive with my laptop and enter them into Excel. The reason for this was to learn what information was contained on each invoice, learn actual prices, transportation costs, and much more. Anyway, upon arriving at this central coop that serviced about thirty-eight member coops, each coop had between fifty and one-hundred members, I found five invoices waiting for me.

I entered them and encouraged the coop representative to go to my presentation on Wednesday. He promised he would, but I understood that he meant that "if it rained, he would go" and we were in the dry season. No rain would arrive for several months. I asked him to step around the desk to see the budget program. He did and I gave him a brief tour. He grabbed a notepad and took notes and started to become more animated. I now felt confident that he would be at the presentation.

From there, we returned to Huambo and took off in another direction to visit some women from a women's coop. They had forty-five members, each with from twelve to forty acres. It was customary here to leave sixty to seventy percent of land resting; therefore, these women supported their families on five to twenty-five acres of cultivated land.

We arrived and three women were waiting for us. We entered the house of one of the ladies. Her house was better than I thought it would be. I had seen so many houses made from mud bricks with dirt floors and tin roofs, but her house had a tile roof (cooler), a cement floor, and had larger rooms than the adobe houses. It was an old house. The bricks were covered with plaster with the plaster falling off in areas and the paint was old, but it was a reasonable house.

The women were very personable and friendly. I took notes on each one's farming operation and we promised to try to help them. We invited them to the presentation which would take place only a couple blocks from this house. No matter what I did in Angola, my main goal was to help these ladies and thousands of women like them.

Wednesday arrived, the day I was to present the results of my investigation into the costs of production, level of risk associated with price and production risk, and other management practices that could be changed to enhance profit.

We drove to the village where the women's coop was located. There was a large building that we could use. The building was circular with a radius of twenty-five feet. The floor was concrete, the walls were bamboo with plenty of open spots to allow air circulation, and the ceiling was tile lying on cross boards. There were no internal poles to hold up the ceiling. The building looked primitive, but to construct such a large building without any internal poles to support the roof suggested that the architecture was advanced.

Someone brought a small generator and set it up. I set up a machine to convert my slides to a screen and we were open for business. Many women came, the director of the university came, several extension agents came, and a newspaper reporter was present. The two large farmers did not come. This demonstrated their level of interest in our work.

The presentation went smoothly and all presenters were impressed with the results. I felt that I had done all that I could under the circumstances.

That evening, I took the two technicians and the driver to my restaurant where I ate chicken every day since my arrival. I introduced them to Brazilian guaraná, a flavor of the soda. They loved it. I bought each of them two cans to take home to share with their families. They ordered goat meat. Not my favorite, but I was tired of chicken and the meal was for them.

The next morning, they were to pick me up at the hotel at 5:45 a.m. My telephone's battery was low, and I did not have the correct adopter to charge it. That was my only alarm clock. I grabbed the telephone that the company gave me to use. I could not get past the pin number. Without a telephone to wake me, I had to awake at 5:15 a.m. without an alarm. I went to bed early. The top half of the bedroom door was glass. I turned on the bathroom light and covered the glass with a towel. The room was lighter and gave me a better chance of awaking.

No problem. I awoke at 5:10 a.m. and was in front of the hotel by 5:20 a.m. It was almost 5:50 a.m. when the driver arrived. I was worried because check-in was at 10:00 a.m. I always worried that I would miss the flight and we had a long drive ahead of us. We arrived at 9:30 a.m. because there was no traffic on the highway. No one was there. I waited at the front of the line. After a few minutes, people scurried in and started moving things around. Soon, other people started dribbling in. They looked at their watches and then at the people running around. After twenty minutes or so, they checked my bags, but they made me check both bags. The smaller one contained my camera, computer, and other important stuff. I cringed, but there was nothing I could do but to leave it in their care.

We sat and waited. I asked my colleagues when the flight should leave. They said, if I am really lucky, it would leave sometime between 10:00 and 12:00 p.m. If I were just lucky, it would leave after 12:00 p.m. If not, it would not leave. I already knew that, but I wanted them to lie to me. Eventually, the plane landed, and was prepared for our flight to Luanda. I said goodbye to my friends and walked toward the plane.

The flight from Kuito to Luanda was uneventful. When we left the plane and found our way into the baggage claim, we had to wait again for what was a long time. When the bags appeared, most were not suitcases, but large plastic bags and baskets filled with food and merchandise. From the spillage, I found they contained potatoes, onions, fresh beef, fresh fish, flour, sugar, and who knows what. The bags were broken, spilling and flowing everywhere. One man told me that on the previous flight, his bag was soaked in blood from fresh beef. He had to destroy it. It was unusable. There was so much food on the flight because food in Huambo was much cheaper than in Luanda.

The trip from Luanda to Johannesburg, on to Atlanta, and then to St. Louis, was uneventful, except for a headache and upset stomach. My head had been aching for a couple of days and my stomach had been very touchy for most of the last sixteen days. There were many moments on airplanes when I thought I would be grabbing the little popcorn bag kept in the pouch behind the next seat and grossing out my fellow passengers. But I did not.

It was now 3:00 a.m., twelve hours into being home. I was completely awake. For me, it was 9:00 a.m. the next morning. I was feeling nothing and was running around the house doing nothing, still high on adrenalin from my trip. My feet hurt beyond belief. I was hungry for food, but I could not eat. My stomach was so confused the last two weeks by such a different diet that it did not know what to do. This was very unusual because I had a cast-iron stomach. Over the years, my stomach was normal while people around me were running into the bushes, but this trip was different.

By 5:00 a.m. I had made chicken soup and madly consumed nearly a gallon of it. I immediately started my recovery. Now, I needed to sleep again. In four hours, I would start a new semester with a new set of faces at the university.

Living in Angola August 2011

This morning, in Johannesburg, I ate a huge breakfast because it only cost fifteen dollars. The same meal in Angola would cost forty dollars, so I must "fill-the-hump." I had a huge plate of yogurt then fruit salad, watermelon, cantaloupe, followed by two eggs with two types of pork. The pork was the best I ever tasted. I followed that with two glasses of the most magnificent orange juice I ever drank. This was my third trip to Angola.

I have had good luck on this trip, except for the last stage. The lady sitting next to me on the plane from Johannesburg to Luanda became ill and started passing out and vomiting as we were preparing to take off. I acted as translator for her to the flight attendants.

On this trip, the Huambo airport was still out of use. CNFA bought me a ticket to Benguela, a small city on the Atlantic coast. The trip to Benguela was uneventful. The driver and agronomist were there to meet me with the pickup. We went to a restaurant to eat before starting the trip to Huambo. There were no cities or restaurants on the way.

This region was arid. The houses were brown from the unpainted adobe used to construct them. The city lacked color and there were no plants, especially trees, in the region. I also noticed how dirty the city was with garbage scattered about.

I saw many Baobab trees along the way. Suddenly, the highway curved and there was a burned-out semi-tractor and trailer planted directly in front of us. There were no warning signs placed along the highway, only the surprise when you rounded the curve. I wondered how many accidents had occurred there, especially at night because of the burnt-out truck.

I was again lodged in a spare room at the CNFA office to save CNFA money. I liked my room there because I was always there when the activities started, and I had a small kitchen where I could fry an egg if I became hungry.

The next morning, I was delivered to the university where I found the new classroom in which the class was to be held. The door was unlocked, and the small whiteboard had markers. I also noticed that there was no echo in this room. I did not know if this was by chance or by design, but I was happy.

The professors and extension agents started to file in. About ten people arrived. Before I started teaching, I went around the room and asked each what they wanted to learn. I learned that most people wanted different things. There was no consensus if I should teach linear regression or analysis of variance. I announced that I would review linear regression for a few days and then show how linear regression and analysis of variance were related. Finally, I would use the rest of the time on analysis of variance. Few people were happy with that, but I saw no alternative under the circumstances.

As the days passed, I found that two or three people were always absent but two or three new people would appear. I don't know how the new people thought they could benefit from class without starting the course from the beginning. I think they only wanted the certificate that would be handed out at the end of the class.

After class ended at 12:30 p.m., we returned to CNFA to have a quick lunch before heading to the first farm to survey the contour lines which would allow the farm owner to build terraces with his plow.

When we arrived, we learned that they had not prepared enough stakes to survey the entire field. I set up the laser instrument that I had brought with me, and we started laying the contour lines until the stakes were gone. I asked the farmer to prepare twice that number of stakes for the next day. He agreed. The farm owner agreed to be present to start to construct the terraces with a plow. I wanted to supervise this step to ensure that they did it correctly.

When we returned the next day to finish the staking, the landowner was not there. In fact, he left word that he could only see us the following week. Next week I was supposed to be working with the women's coop and the large coop, so that did not work for me. I was beginning to think that we were wasting our time working with the two brothers. They gave the appearance that they knew everything and thought that the purpose of our meetings was for them to teach us. Although I am sure we could learn from them, we also could help them increase their profits greatly.

We drove to the field to continue our surveying. We found that the stakes we had left the day before had been removed. At first, I thought that grazing cattle had knocked them over, but upon closer examination, we saw that the stakes were missing. After a brief investigation, we learned that when the women were returning yesterday after work, they spied the stakes and thought that they were the perfect size for their evening cooking files. They walked down each row and removed them. We had to redo everything.

We resurveyed the area and replaced the old stakes with new ones. The man cutting the stakes was responsible to spread the word that the women were to leave our stakes in peace. We returned to Huambo for supper.

The next day we returned to the large coop property. They had a large field that was suffering great erosion. We talked the coop director into allowing us to survey the field for contour terraces. I tried to convince him to have a tractor and plow there in the field so that they could immediately start constructing the terraces. For some reason, that was not possible.

The day was extremely hot, and I exhausted my water supply quickly. We had to survey part of the field twice to make sure that we had it right. After three hours, I was dying from thirst, but we finished the staking. I explained to the director how the tractor and plow should be used to make the terraces. We finished and drove back to Huambo. I had this feeling in my stomach that not one terrace was going to be built. I think they allowed me to stake the fields so that I would feel good. I don't think either landowner intended to construct a terrace. If I were to demonstrate the benefits from farming on the contour, we would need to find the right landowner who would follow through on the project on some future trips.

On the way back to Huambo, we were detained at a traffic stop. Unfortunately, when I changed pants that morning, I did not transfer my passport to my clean pants. The police were going to fine me for traveling without my passport. We tried to talk our way around it but to no avail. Finally, my colleague offered the policeman a bribe. Suddenly, our problem disappeared, and we were cleared to continue.

Finally, my trip was over, and I prepared to return to Luanda via Benguela. We left for Benguela in the pickup. We arrived around noon, ate, and they dropped me at the airport. They waited for me to catch my flight before they started back to Huambo.

When we returned to Huambo, I went to the market to look for souvenirs. What I found was a coffee crusher. This was part of a tree trunk that was hollowed out on one end. Coffee beans were placed in this hole and then crushed with a stick. I also found a four-foot pounding stick that was two inches in diameter and four feet long. It was made from hardwood. It was heavy, even so, I bought them both. I envisioned placing them in my office at Southern Illinois University at Edwardsville and wowing my students.

I arrived in Huambo and went straight to my hotel room. I had to spend the night in Luanda so that I could catch the flight to Johannesburg the next morning. Once I was settled in and figured out how to pack the tree trunk, I headed to the streets to walk around. I was starting to become hungry. I thought I might sit in a nice street bar. What I found was that Angola, unlike Brazil, almost had no bars and I had to walk forever to find a street bar.

In Angola, beer was cheaper than water and I needed to economize my money. Once I found the bar, I ordered a beer. I sipped it slowly and watched people. The traffic was a continuous jam. People were walking both ways. Some carried things on their heads; others carried the merchandise they were selling in their hands. Still, others were running or walking. I watched as darkness crept over the city and lights appeared.

I finished my first beer and waited for the waitress to come and ask me if I wanted another beer. She did not come. I was the only person sitting in the bar. For only one person to be drinking on a sidewalk bar is unthinkable in Brazil. In Angola, it did not guarantee service. The lady ignored me. Finally, I waved my hand and asked for another beer. She brought it and was pleasant, but immediately disappeared. After I finished that beer, I waited for her to notice that I was ready for another. I waited an hour. It did not happen. When I was tired of watching people, I asked her for the bill. It was 170 kwanzas. I gave her 200 kwanzas. Surprise, surprise! She did not have change. This was going to be her tip. I waited for my chance. After a few minutes, she came to the table and asked if I had understood what she had said. I confirmed that I did and that I was only waiting for my change. She again said she did not have it. I suggested that since she owed me thirty kwanzas, all she had to do was to give me a fifty. She asked if I had a twenty to make a change. I responded that I did not have change but then I would only owe her twenty kwanzas. That was better than their owing me thirty kwanzas. She frowned and quickly disappeared. Shortly she reappeared with the exact change.

The next morning, I dragged my loot to the airport and stood in the check-in line. When I reached the front, they saw my bean-crushing pole and asked me to open my luggage. I did and they found the hollowed-out tree trunk. They asked to see a document that was issued by the Department of Tourism which would state that my present was not a national treasure, which by law could not leave the country. I tried to reason with them, but they would not budge. I removed the tree trunk from my bag and took it to the middle of the airport floor and carefully placed it upright. I made a second trip to place the crushing pole beside it. The rest of my trip was uneventful.

Living in Guyana: September 15, 2019—The Trip

I had been nervous for days about this trip to Guyana--a country where I had never been before. Normally, I would be excited about these events, but this time I was worried. I worried that my car might have a flat time in the three-hour drive to the airport; I worried that my old car might decide to cash in its chips on the way; I worried that my bad feet would painfully cramp on me during the two flights: St. Louis to Miami and

Miami to Georgetown, Guyana; I worried that my big fat body would not fit into the ever-smaller seating space on airlines, and; I worried that my ever-increasing age might limit my ability to move about once I was in the country. I worried a lot.

I was comforted that my good friend from work shadowed me for the three-hour drive to where I could stash my car near the airport (twenty-five miles away), and then he graciously took me to the airport. I worried about retrieving my electronic ticket from the ticket machine, but it also behaved with the help of a kind lady who worked for the airline. I reached the security check where they took my suntan lotion and mosquito spray, but; otherwise, I made it through and found my gate.

The flight was full, which caused a shortage of overhead bin space, so I checked my carry-on bag after I removed my camera. I boarded and found that I had an aisle seat, which anyone who is overweight and with a bladder the size of a peanut would appreciate.

The trip to Miami was quick and calm. I found which gate my connecting flight was and made the long haul to that gate in good time. Upon sitting down at the gate, I received a text telling me the new gate number, which was back about the same distance. The universe was conspiring for me to get back into good physical condition.

Somewhere during the flight, a flight attendant handed out a customs document for everyone to fill out. I looked at it and I could not read a single word. The printing was so small. I flagged the flight attendant and she promised to help me fill it in later.

The connecting flight was full. I sat next to a Scottish seaman who was being flown to Georgetown to connect with a sea vessel for his new assignment. The flight was four and a half hours, modest relative to many flights that I had made, but still a worry for my cramping feet. I had missed taking pills for the pain because they had been stored in the carry-on suitcase that I unexpectedly checked. I kept moving my feet about under the seat to relieve the pain. Eventually, I got out of my aisle seat and moved to the rear of the plane to spend some time standing. We were still only midway to Georgetown. The flight attendant came and helped me fill out my customs sheet, but I could not remember the address of the hotel where I would stay. She decided to leave it blank.

My bladder was filling. I considered using the restroom on board, but they often become dirty on longer flights and I tried to hold it. I was certain that I could do it. As soon as we landed, I could scoot into the many restroom facilities and take care of business. As the flight droned on, I was revisiting my decision to hold it, but I did.

We landed and, instead of being dropped off into the nice tube that walks us into the airport, we were dumped onto the tarmac where we had to walk about two football fields. I struggled. I was not used to everyone passing me, including little old ladies with canes. Once inside we entered long lines where we had to wait for customs agents to stamp our passports, and they were slow. It took forever to process even a few people. Meanwhile, my bladder was screaming.

Finally, it was my turn to be processed. The young lady scrutinized my documents and asked me in what hotel was I staying. I repeated that I could not remember the address. She decided to refer me to her supervisor. My bladder was tightening. The supervisor was himself processing a passenger and asked me to wait. My bladder was not happy. After a couple minutes he motioned for me to follow him and he charged outside the building to ask my driver where I was staying. I struggled to keep pace with him. Finally, we located my driver and satisfied the supervisor. He approved me to leave. I had to reenter the building, find my luggage, and return to the driver.

I was optimistic that I would soon be in my hotel and could relax my bladder. As the driver reached to help me with my bags, I asked how far to the hotel. He responded that it was an hour's drive away. My bladder reacted by causing me to spurt out, "No, not an hour!" I calmed myself and convinced myself that I could handle it. I just had to keep talking and take my mind from it.

As my driver drove, I asked him questions. I learned that Guyana had a good future due to new oil discoveries, but his optimism was controlled due to the behavior of politicians. They were known to make questionable decisions and to make statements that created racial tension between the two main races: Black and Indian (from India).

His driving was excellent; although, I cannot say the same for the other drivers. They tended to follow other cars at no more than ten feet before passing. Being a former British colony, they drove on the left side of the road, which was strange.

When we reached the hotel, I was happy, but also exhausted, hot, and sweaty. I entered a vacant office area. It was 1:30 AM. No one was present, but there was a bell. I rang the bell. No one came. My bladder urged me to keep ringing it until I heard some noise from behind a door.

A sleepy man came out. He asked me my name and if I had a reservation. I did. He started punching keys on a computer that was hidden from my view. He looked at me and we waited, and waited, and waited. He smiled. I asked why he couldn't process me so I could go to my room. He said he was waiting for the computer to power up.

I was almost crying from desperation. Finally, he started typing and found me in the system, and gave me a room key. He typed something else and then disappeared into the back room. I started looking for a dark corner of the room. The printer jumped to life and printed a page. The man reappeared, collected the paper, and handed it to me on top of the counter. He gave me a pen and asked me to fill it in. I gave up all hope. My bladder was exploding. I was hot, sweating like a fool, and uncomfortable, but I filled out the paper.

He called in the man to help me carry my luggage to my room. At last, relief was around the corner. We walked outside and around the corner and he pointed to stairs and offered for me to lead the way. I held back and told him to show me the way. He grabbed my two suitcases and jumped up the stairs. I struggled. On the first floor, he disappeared around a corner. When I reached the top of the first stairs, I saw the man at the top of the second stack of stairs. He smiled and disappeared around the corner. I uttered profanity. Finally, I made it to the top of the third floor where my room was located. I think that when I woke up the man and asked him to hurry up, he decided to give the old-fat-guy-with-a-beard a room on the top floor—just for giggles.

As he opened the door, I envisioned myself not thinking about my bladder and throwing myself on my bed in a cool room and sleeping deeply. That was when he swung open the door and the overwhelmingly hot air from the room hit me. I could see the toilet since the bathroom door was open. The attendant entered the room, sat down my bags, plugged in the air conditioner, and turned it on, plugged in the television set and that was when I asked him to leave. I could wait no longer. He left the room and I comforted myself.

I laid down on the bed and tried to sleep, but I was sweating profusely, as old-fat-people do. I twisted and turned until the room cooled a bit and exhaustion caught up with me. I was in Guyana.

Living in Guyana— September 20, 2019

Sleep came quickly on my first night, even though I was sweaty, and it was still hot despite the little air conditioner chugging away. I awoke to the ringing of the phone. It was the kitchen wanting to know if I wanted to eat. Apparently, I was the only resident who had not eaten. It was 10:30 A.M. and I was still exhausted. Reluctantly I climbed out of the bed and into the shower.

I quickly dressed and rushed to the dining hall. The attendant lady asked what I wanted to eat. She suggested an omelet with cheese. I agreed. While I waited, she brought me a glass of fresh juice that I sampled. It was delicious. I asked what it was. She responded with a smile that it was watermelon with pineapple. Then the food arrived. It was French fries with fried fish. I usually did not eat fish. I was disappointed. Later, I learned that I had to pay nine dollars for the meal. Then, I was doubly disappointed.

My ride was waiting impatiently for me. I had to go with him to meet with the organization's director. After a short ride on narrow back streets, each surrounded by ditches full of water, we arrived at the director's office. I was extremely impressed with both the director and my colleague, the agronomist-driver. They were organized. We discussed in detail what they expected me to achieve on this visit. I was to spend Tuesday through Thursday visiting farmers and collecting their production data on vegetable production. It would include farmers producing in the field, in shade houses (greenhouses covered with clear plastic and netting to soften the powerful Guyana sun. With this data, I was to create simulation models in

Excel to accommodate as many production systems as possible. Starting on Friday, I was to start training groups of producers on the simulation results. I was also to create a manual record-keeping system so that producers can track their own costs without a computer.

After our meeting, which ended about 1:00 P.M., my driver/colleague/sponsor/guide, drove me to a little, simple establishment to eat. They offered a reduced number of choices of meat, several different kinds of rice, and a few simple salads. We told them what we wanted, and they filled our plate. I selected chicken and rice. The lady overloaded my plate and then piled the chicken on top of it. The chicken was a leg and thigh. The plate cost nine dollars, the same as my breakfast. After we ate, I was dropped off at my hotel. I climbed the stairs very slowly and, upon reaching my bed, I turned on the air conditioner and slept.

On Tuesday, we left the hotel at 7:00 A.M., before the restaurant opened. We drove on narrow roads crowded with people, buses loading and unloading, horses pulling wagons, vans, and huge, I mean HUGE, trucks. Jermaine, my driving colleague, had to manage these obstacles while trying to reach our destination on time. He was a master at driving in his environment.

Despite all the obstacles, Guyana drivers were courteous.

We reached our destination at a tienda located far off the main road. After calling her on her cell phone, Jermaine informed her that we had arrived. Seconds later, an older woman made her way out of the barrier made of iron bars that protected her house and tienda. We sat down and I started to collect data. It was difficult because I had to convert what they said to specific quantities and prices and that was not easy. It was like pulling teeth. This was not because she was being difficult, but that she had never thought of her business in these terms.

By noon, we had collected all the information possible. I was fearful that I had overlooked important pieces, but I would know that later when I was creating the simulation model in Excel. Jermaine found a restaurant and we ate. He left me at the hotel about 2:00 P.M. and I started the work of creating the simulation model.

On Wednesday, we visited several farmers in another region of Guyana. Their types of production varied from shade houses made from salvaged wood. I was certain that any strong wind would blow them over. Even so, he produced lettuce and generated income for his family. Others had sophisticated hydroponic systems for producing vegetables that would withstand most storms. I was impressed with the potential that this system of producing vegetables had for helping develop the rural areas of Guyana.

We arrived at the hotel at 3:00 P.M. and I continued to develop the simulation model. What I had done the first day was not working. I would have to develop a different approach. I worked until late that night to find it. I was worried. I already had a training session scheduled for 10:00 A.M. Friday. I needed to have this developed by then.

On Thursday, we visited a group of producers in the morning, and to my disappointment, we visited another group in the afternoon. I did not return to the hotel until 5:00 P.M. and I was exhausted. I took a nap and continued my work on the simulation model. After I had done all that my eyes would allow me to do, I grabbed my thumb drive and looked for the files that I had prepared before I left the US for data collection forms. These forms were to be used in each shade house to document each time anyone applied material to the vegetables or harvested crops from them. When I left the US, I had grabbed the wrong thumb drive. I did not have the files! I would have to create them again!

It was already late at night when I started to think about the design the collection forms should take. It was helpful to have already seen many different types of production (in the ground, growing boxes outside, growing boxes in shade houses, and hydroponic growing in shade houses). I could easily create the data collection sheets. After an hour I had designed three sheets that should collect all the necessary data. Two would be placed on clipboards in the growing houses and one would be kept in the office. The system was simplistic; yet, complete. I smiled and went to bed.

Friday was the day I had dreaded because I had to present my simulation model, with likely defects. After all, they had been no time to check thoroughly for errors. This first presentation was to a group of young community members lead by a wise old man. The old man, Mr. Michaely, looked like a common old man. He had a short white beard with short white hair. He was missing a tooth or two and had difficulty walking, but he was a leader. He had found these youth and took them under his apprenticeship. He obtained a monetary loan and built a thirty by eighty feet shade house that was strong and that would last many years. Somehow, they shared the work and the revenue; however, so far, all revenues over expenses were placed in a bank account to be reinvested. They were resolved to expand the scale of their operation so that six families could make a living from it.

Mr. Michaely always allowed his youth to make decisions and have input into the decision-making process. I was impressed. They had a computer and knew how to use Excel. One member was more adept at using Excel and would be assigned to using the simulation model as soon as it becomes available to them.

In other circumstances, Mr. Michaely could have been a CEO of a large corporation. He was that capable.

As I made my presentation to the group, even in the heat, they were following every step. Mr. Michaely had me show different parts of the model several times as he struggled to understand it and to check my numbers. He was kind enough to show me a couple of places where there was likely a mistake in my formulas. At one point, he had the "aah ha" moment and said, "We can use this even for crops that we do not produce, and we can take this to the banker to convince him to loan us money for a new crop." I was proud to explain the purpose of a simulation model. It could also be used to calculate the costs and revenues of a crop using best practices and obtaining the best results. He could then compare his actual results from his recordkeeping system to understand how much room there was for him to improve his system of production.

I was proud that they thought that the simulation model was good; although, they emphasized that it had to be easy to use. That was a challenge because it must be complex to be able to receive data from all the different types of production units and still be easy to use. The data collection forms impressed him and his group because they were simple to use. I relaxed and began to feel myself become tired. I had not embarrassed myself at my first training session.

Survival precedes excellence, and I had survived!

We collected our material and headed home. I had the rest of Friday, Saturday, Sunday, and Monday to prepare for my next training session.

Living in Guyana – Saturday Night September 21, 2019

This morning, I was up early and working on the simulation model. When I grew bored of this, I switched to the data collection forms. I made sure that each form occupied a full page. They were ready to be printed and copied for the farmers to use. Then I paced the floor in my room. There was nothing to do. The programs on the television were old and they had the volume capped so that no one could disturb their neighbor. I simply could not hear the television, so it was useless to me.

As the morning passed, I lowered the temperature on the air conditioner. It became hot fast here. I had started to sweat already with the air conditioning doing all that I could make it do. I returned to the computer and finished another two or three producer costs of production scenarios. Each one introduced a new problem that had to be introduced into the simulation model. Little by little, it was becoming better.

Finally, I decided that it was Saturday and that I needed to do something special. I dressed and walked to the poolside bar and ordered a piña colada. It tasted good and put a smile on my face. No one else was by the poolside so I decided to walk down the block to a bar and restaurant located on the second story. It had no walls, so the breeze blew and cooled me down. I ordered the same drink. It was much more expensive and not as good. There were only a few old men there discussing local politics. I decided to leave. I asked the bartender for directions to another bar that might show more activity. He called a cab for me.

When I arrived at the place, I entered and could not see, the bar was very dark. I paused a moment for my eyes to adjust. There was horrible rap music playing loudly with people everywhere, drinking and happily talking. I had no more than ordering a drink when a woman approached me and asked if I wanted company. I liked to talk, so I invited her to sit at my table.

She was a refugee from Venezuela, where the country was experiencing horrible times with food difficult to find.

She said that most of the girls who worked in the bar were from Venezuela and that most of her family was still in Venezuela. She was saving money to help them escape into Guyana, which was stable and peaceful. After a beer, I left. I was too old and too poor for such entertainment experiences.

I enjoyed these experiences with the varied people I met. At the hotel, there was a security guard. He told me that he worked twelve hours a day and six days a week. That was the nature of his job. That was what he did to make a living for his family. There was no overtime pay. He was a friendly gentleman and greeted me warmly each time I left and returned.

Yesterday, he must have been off or sick. I missed him when I did not see him at his station.

Living in Guyana-- September 24, 2019

I had spent most part of the last four days in my room working on improving the simulation model and the record-keeping system. There was always something to do to tweak it. I found that this trip was not full of adventure. I did not see much of Guyana; although, I had a good sample of what it was like to live there. The people were kind, courteous, and intelligent. Even the vehicle drivers on the congested streets were courteous. I found that it was not bad to be held up in my room for so much time because I had my bed for naps and an air conditioner to cool me down. I could also go to the bar and buy a soda if I so desired.

What I noticed was that there was no French bread in Guyana and people did not drink coffee. Those who did, drank instant coffee. Having lived ten years in Brazil, French bread and coffee were essential for breakfast and for mid-afternoon snacks. Tea and sliced bread did not have the same effect.

I also noticed that I had only seen one bakery. In Eastern Europe and Latin America, Guyana excluded, I saw bakeries on almost every corner. The same went for pharmacies. I saw only one pharmacy in Guyana; although they must exist, I did not see them.

I loved chatting with the lady who came daily to tidy my room. She was of Indian heritage. I struggled to understand her English, but that did not slow her down. She confidently told me of her hopes to visit the US next year. She would do so by herself because she was no longer married. She told me of her daughter, who was a lawyer, and much more. This was done while she busily made my bed and swept the floor. She seemed to me to be a lonely woman who worked hard at making a living as a single person.

On Sunday, the pool was filled with people laughing, splashing, and screaming. It was the sound of pure happiness. Three female hotel staff members were making drinks and taking food orders. They always had big smiles on their faces. I thought that any woman with a smile that originated in their soul was beautiful. All three of these workers were beautiful. They had their long hair neatly tied into a bun on the top of their heads. They were neat, clean, and efficient.

A man came and set up a table and placed something that played music on it. The music had the Caribbean beat. Surprise! As soon as he turned on the music, the staff members and guests started to walk while moving to the beat of the music. I drank my piña colada and watched the beauty as it unfolded before me. There was no more beautiful sight in the world than a Latin woman (or the Caribbean) dancing to her music. Like her smile, the moves started down in her soul and just magically came out. She was not aware of what she was doing. Her body just did it.

Last night (Monday), I went to the bar to order a snack to avoid the middle of the night hunger attacks. A couple was watching a horror movie on the TV. They were snuggling like they were in their living room. Only one female staff member was working. She did not smile. I ordered my food and started watching the horror film. Another man appeared and fluttered around from the bar to share the chairs while watching the TV. He seemed distracted. He went and talked to the bar supervisor, a heavy-set man who moved about the area. Minutes later, the man took the TV controls and changed the channel from the movie that three people were watching to a cricket match. The couple got up and left. I could not believe that I ate my snack while watching a cricket match.

My driver and technical advisor fetched me today for lunch. The place we ate in Georgetown was simple, but it had wonderful food and an air-conditioned room. We always had a choice of pork or chicken with two or three types of rice and two fresh fruit drinks. I always selected passion fruit. After we ate, my partner liked to sip his drink slowly and allow the food to settle. Today he started to talk. He talked about Guyana's political problems. Unfortunately, they were much the same as the US was experiencing. He voiced concerns that the small farmers' problems were not so much from not knowing how to produce vegetables as their difficulties marketing their vegetables after they were produced. My friend was also a small producer and spoke from experience.

Tomorrow, I will have my second training session. I have revamped both the simulation model and the data entry forms, plus I completed a brief statistical analysis of five years monthly prices for tomatoes and Pak choi. I know. I had no idea what Pak choi was either.

Living in Guyana-- September 25, 2019

I awoke early today to leave by 6:45 A.M. I had a training session in a village ninety miles south of Georgetown. The idea was to avoid as much traffic congestion as possible. We failed. The traffic was horrible most of the way. It took three hours to travel the ninety miles. We were halfway to our destination when the local leader called to say that no one could attend our presentation. My colleague told me that the local leader had not done his job and had not taken the time to invite the group members to our presentation. He was all talk and no action. Germaine, my colleague, said that we would continue and find as many members as possible and individually make my presentation.

After three hours we arrived at our first house. Our first group member was a young grandmother and businesswoman. We were invited to sit down on benches outside the tienda she ran out of the front of her house. I set up my laptop computer on my lap, but it kept slipping off. She and Germaine disappeared into the house and returned with a small table that I used to support the computer.

I took her through the simulation model, and she corrected a few of my numbers that were relevant to her operation. She agreed that the numbers were reasonable. I showed her the record-keeping forms and she also agreed that they were reasonable. I then showed her my analysis for the prices of tomatoes and another vegetable that I had never heard of. She asked for copies of my files. She owned a computer and was Excel literate.

As soon as we were done with business, she produced two fresh, green coconuts for us to drink the water. It was delicious. That was the first time I had drunk fresh coconut water since I left Natal, Brazil in 1984. Then she produced two warm pastries that she had prepared. After we had finished and we were leaving, I extended my hand to shake her hand. She brushed it aside and pulled me in for a hug. That alone made the trip worthwhile.

We tried to find other producers at home, but we failed. There was nothing to do but return to Georgetown. I had a severe headache by this time and was ready to be returned to my hotel where I had my stash of Excedrin.

Tomorrow, we would leave at 7:00 A.M to conduct one training session in the morning and another in the afternoon. I would take the Excedrin with me.

Living in Guyana--September 26, 2019

We left again at 7:00 A.M. today. We fought heavy traffic, but since we were only traveling fifteen miles, or so, it only took an hour to arrive. We had to round up the coop members one by one by visiting their houses. It took a one-half hour to get them to the coop building. There we waited for the coop President to arrive with the key to open the building.

When he opened the building, I started searching for a place to use as a screen to project upon with our portable overhead projector. I did not find any area. The entire room was bright making it difficult for the coop members to see anything that we projected. After some discussion, the coop members grabbed three or four wooden benches and a small plywood square that served as a blackboard. They started out the door and across to the neighbor's house.

I followed.

They quickly arranged the benches and tried to set up the blackboard on top of one bench, but it kept falling. Ultimately, I was set up under a tree in the front yard of a house with my computer on a table and the coop members trying to see my computer screen. They said they could see, but I knew they could not see. I made my presentation by describing the screens to them rather than showing the screens to them. I had to be flexible.

In the end, the farmers understood and appreciated what I said. They asked for copies of the files on their thumb drives. I gladly shared my files. I never expected these farmers to be computer literate, but many were.

It was hot and humid. I was sweating profusely. My shirt stuck to my skin and was wet. My face was sweating so much that I had to wipe it dry with my handkerchief. I was grateful when we reached the pickup and turned on the air conditioner.

We reached Georgetown again by 11:00 A.M. My colleague dropped me off at my hotel. He said he would pick me up at 2:00 P.M. for a 3:00 P.M. meeting. I was starving, so I ordered food, and after I ate, I took a brief nap, my alarm sounded, I dressed and descended into the heat to wait for my colleague. The sun was hot, even in the shade. I immediately started to sweat. After several minutes, my colleague came to tell me that the meeting had been delayed an hour and that he would return in an hour to pick me up. I climbed my steep stairs and laid down again to wait.

My colleague arrived, picked me up, and we started for our last presentation. It was close so it only took a few minutes to arrive. Our destination was a primary school. We waited several minutes for the coop members to arrive, and we entered the building. The room was large and hot. There was no air conditioning and no breeze.

I was sweating profusely at once, but then, that was what old fat men do. Germaine and I set up our equipment. We pulled a table out and set up the projector at the appropriate distance from the wall. I started my computer. I encouraged the coop members to come closer to the wall so they could read the Excel model. They declined. I tried to make the print as large as possible and we started the presentation. At first, they showed no interest in what I was talking about. I think they were tired and were struggling to stay awake in the heat. I tried to involve them in the discussion, but they kept comments to a minimum. Finally, I finished my presentation. That was when I was able to draw them into a conversation. They did like what I presented; although, they recognized that it will take their dedication to start and finish a bookkeeping system on their farms.

Germaine and I started for Georgetown, but we ran into traffic. Our trip took much more than an hour when it only took twenty minutes to come. Tomorrow I must complete my final report and then all I must do is to wait for my plane to leave early Sunday morning. It was a good trip.

CPSIA information can be obtained
at www.ICGtesting.com
Printed in the USA
JSHW050837081221
21049JS00006B/128